TAOISM FOR BEGINNERS

Understanding and Applying
Taoist History, Concepts, and Practices

TAOISM
FOR BEGINNERS

ELIZABETH RENINGER

ROCKRIDGE
PRESS

Interior & Cover Designer: Liz Cosgrove
Art Producer: Sara Feinstein
Editor: Lia Ottaviano
Production Editor: Matthew Burnett

Illustrations used under license from iStock.com.

ISBN: Print 978-1-64152-542-8 | eBook 978-1-64152-543-5

R0

Dedicated to my teachers and friends
along the Way.

CONTENTS

INTRODUCTION

TAOISM is one of China's three main spiritual traditions and has been around for thousands of years. Its multitude of lineages, ceremonies, philosophies, and practices make it immensely complex. The good news is that this book provides an easy-to-follow map to this rich territory. Here, I will offer a clear and straightforward overview of Taoism's core concepts, basic teachings, historical lineages, and foundational practices. You'll get a taste of the full spectrum of Taoist disciplines without being buried in a mountain of minutiae.

Since you've picked up this book, chances are good that you feel interested, intrigued, or perhaps just a bit curious about this particular spiritual tradition. And, as it turns out, there is, indeed, much of interest—a veritable wealth of information and insights—for you to explore. So, welcome to this beginner's guide to Taoism! Here's what lies ahead:

Chapter one introduces the key figures and primary texts of Taoism. It also discusses the relationship between Taoism and China's other two spiritual traditions: Confucianism and Buddhism.

In **chapters two** and **three**, I'll present the concepts and teachings central to Taoist practice and worldview. What is Tao? What is *ch'i*? What's the meaning of *yin* and *yang*? What are the Three Treasures of Taoism? This basic vocabulary will help you navigate, with comfort and skill, the terrain of Taoist practice.

Chapter four introduces the deities, temples, and rituals associated with ceremonial Taoism. It also provides a glimpse of Taoist divination systems such as *feng shui* and the *I Ching*.

In **chapter five**, I'll debunk some common myths and misconceptions about Taoism. In **chapter six**, I'll present an overview of various Taoist lineages. And in **chapter seven**, I'll offer specific guidance on how to begin your own Taoist practice.

Throughout the text—in sidebars titled "Everyday Taoism"—I will provide step-by-step guidance for exercises, meditations, and experiments that will help you incorporate Taoist principles into your daily activities.

Elizabeth's Taoism Journey

I first learned about Taoism via an undergraduate "survey of religions" class. Truth be told, I don't remember much about this class except that it sparked what would become a lifelong interest in exploring the commonalities as well as differences among various spiritual paths.

My first actual engagement with Taoist practices came while I was studying Chinese medicine. Along with acupuncture, herbal medicine, and *tuina* (meridian-based massage), my course of study included *ch'i kung*.

Ch'i kung is a kind of Taoist yoga with roots in ancient China. It involves the cultivation of life-force energy and plays a central role in Taoist inner alchemy. It's also the internal (i.e., mind, breath, and subtle energy) practice associated with all of the martial arts.

Immediately, I fell in love with the ch'i kung practice, and it has been part of my life ever since. The Taoist celebration of the natural world, its appreciation of spontaneity and paradox, and its invitation to live our lives in deep harmony with the flowing patterns of the universe are principles that I continue to greatly value and do my best to embody.

I look forward to serving as your guide, offering glimpses of the vast spiritual terrain of Taoism, and introducing practices with immediate relevance to your daily life—and to the life and continuing harmony of our shared planet.

A Note on Transliteration

There are two transliteration systems currently in use for Romanizing Chinese characters and rendering them into words using the English alphabet. As a result, there are two spellings of many words associated with Taoist practice. For instance:

- Tao (via the older Wade-Giles transliteration system) and Dao (via the newer pinyin system)

- Taoist (Wade-Giles) and Daoist (pinyin)

- Ch'i (Wade-Giles) and Qi (pinyin)

- Ch'i Kung (Wade-Giles) and Qigong (pinyin)

- T'ai Chi (Wade-Giles) and Taiji (pinyin)

In this book, I'll be using the Wade-Giles system with pinyin spellings sometimes added parenthetically the first time a term is introduced. Please see the Appendix (page 145) for a chart displaying side-by-side Wade-Giles and pinyin spellings of many Taoist terms.

ONE

What Is Taoism?

*A journey of a thousand miles begins with the
first step.*

You're likely familiar with this phrase, which provides
some excellent advice and encouragement for beginning any new venture.

But did you know that these words are attributed
to the Taoist sage Lao Tzu? They appear in the 64th
chapter of the *Tao Te Ching,* the most well-known of all
Taoist texts. Here's the same passage in a slightly more
expanded form with a slightly different translation:

*The giant pine tree
grows from a tiny sprout.
The journey of a thousand miles
starts from beneath your feet.*
(TRANSLATION BY STEPHEN MITCHELL)

1

As you begin your journey through this book, you might imagine yourself as a tiny sprout, trusting that a regal pine tree already exists within you. Before you know it (and with the help of a bit of rain and sunshine), you'll have completed the journey.

What's also worth keeping in mind, however, is that the descriptions I'll offer here—like the illustrations and contour lines on a topographic map—can only show you the right direction; they are never a substitute for actually entering and experiencing the territory yourself. In other words: The map is not the territory!

Lao Tzu himself acknowledges this in the very first chapter of the *Tao Te Ching*:

> The tao that can be told
> is not the eternal Tao
> The name that can be named
> is not the eternal Name.
> The unnamable is the eternally real.
> Naming is the origin
> of all particular things.
>
> (TRANSLATION BY STEPHEN MITCHELL)

Don't worry if this seems a bit paradoxical or hard to grasp. It will become clearer as you make your way through the book and explore for yourself the actual territory of Taoist practice via the exercises and meditations that I'll offer along the way.

In this first chapter, you'll learn a bit about Taoism's history and what makes it unique among spiritual traditions. You'll be introduced to Taoism's two most esteemed sages: Lao Tzu and Chuang Tzu. You'll learn how Taoism's scriptures and philosophical texts are organized and which of these are the most well-known.

And finally, you'll be offered a glimpse of how China's other two religious traditions—Buddhism and Confucianism—are related to Taoism.

What Is Taoism?

Taoism is a religious tradition that originated in China about 2,500 years ago, during what was known as China's Classical period. For this reason, its first texts comprise what is now referred to as Classical Taoism. Since that time, the Taoist tradition has gone through a multitude of transformations, including being transplanted into Western cultures.

In Western popular culture, the images and activities associated with Taoism include:

- Enjoying martial arts movies such as *Enter the Dragon* (featuring Bruce Lee) and *Crouching Tiger, Hidden Dragon* (directed by Ang Lee)

- Taking a *t'ai chi* or *ch'i kung* class to improve your health

- Using feng shui principles to reorganize your home or office

- Consulting the *I Ching* for help in making an important decision

While many people in Western cultures participate in such activities, fewer are aware of their Taoist origins. And this isn't necessarily a problem. We can benefit from ch'i kung or feng shui and enjoy a good martial arts film without knowing anything about their historical roots.

But for those of us interested in understanding Taoism more deeply, we need to move beyond the vague impression that this spiritual tradition is simply about learning how to "go with the flow." We need to move beyond fanciful notions of becoming a badass martial artist or Taoist wizard performing magical feats or of living in a remote mountain cave as a Taoist hermit.

While these popular opinions hold a kernel of truth, Taoism, as you'll see, is so much more!

Taoism's Contemporary Appeal

The contemporary appeal of Taoist principles actually makes a lot of sense. The environmental challenges our planet is now facing (via global warming, etc.) make Taoism's deep respect and reverence for the natural world a potentially powerful resource. It's a worldview that can support us in reversing our currently destructive trends and restoring some measure of harmony.

And there are many aspects of Taoist practice that can enhance physical and psychological comfort, ease, and relaxation. This can be a welcome balm for those of us living in fast-paced cultures or working in high-stress professions. A Taoist approach to our day-to-day living can go far in supporting our overall well-being.

Like any spiritual path, Taoism speaks most deeply to that part of us that yearns for lasting peace and joy—for a kind of happiness that is not tethered to the comings and goings of the mundane world. This appeal has less to do with our current circumstances. It is rooted, instead, in the mysterious "place" from which any spiritual journey both begins and ends.

Whether your interest in Taoism stems from concern for the global environment or a desire to enhance your physical and mental-emotional health or a yearning for spiritual insight, you're in the right place!

What Makes Taoism Unique?

In many ways, Taoism is quite similar to other religious traditions. There are rituals and ceremonies. There's a pantheon of deities and saints. There's an absolute principle (Tao) that informs all human experience. There are scriptures and philosophical texts that articulate its teachings. These characteristics can be found in many other spiritual traditions.

Like all spiritual traditions, Taoism has an institutional as well as a contemplative aspect. The institutional aspect includes its temples, its hierarchy of Taoist priests, and its rituals and ceremonies. It also includes its canon of scriptures, treatises, and texts, and martial arts and alchemy lineages and techniques.

The contemplative or esoteric aspect of Taoism refers to the *subjective experience* of its practitioners: the insights and intuitions that arise in the course of their engagement with Taoist ritual, meditation, or inner alchemy.

Like all religious traditions, Taoism's various organizational forms have a twofold purpose. Most essentially, they're designed to nourish and unfold subjective experience, the mystical heart of the practice. They're also designed to impart various practical benefits.

Like most spiritual traditions, Taoism also has a cosmology: a story of how the universe came into existence and how it maintains or transforms itself moment by moment.

And like most religious traditions, Taoism has a soteriology: a theory of how spiritual liberation—the ultimate goal of the tradition—is attained. This is Taoism's road map, showing the way from ignorance and dis-ease to wisdom, harmony, and enlightenment—from emotional turmoil, confusion, and dissatisfaction to inner peace.

You'll learn a lot more about Taoism's cosmology and soteriology in upcoming chapters.

But for now, let's explore what makes Taoism unique among religious traditions. What gives it its characteristic flavor? This uniqueness has a lot to do with these three central tenets:

1. **A reverence for the natural world.** Taoist practice remains intimately involved with the elements of the natural world. Spiritual insight and liberation are not separate from, but rather deeply interwoven with, the rhythms and changing patterns of nature.

2. **A respect for physical health and longevity.** Taoism understands the macrocosm of the universe to be reflected in the microcosm of the human body. In inner alchemy practice in particular, the human body becomes a vessel within which the Three Treasures (essence, vitality, and spirit) are cultivated. The human body is—at least potentially—a temple of the divine.

3. **An insightful understanding of opposites.** Taoism's yin-yang theory provides a revolutionary way of relating to pairs of opposites. Rather than being mutually exclusive, pairs of opposites are understood to always arise *interdependently*, with each containing the essence of the other. More on this later.

道 EVERYDAY TAOISM: DISCOVERING YOUR TRUE BODY

One of Taoism's essential insights is that the microcosm of our human body-mind is a mirror image of the macrocosm of the entire cosmos. This exercise will help you get a sense of this.

1. Find a place to sit quietly for a few minutes.

2. Close your eyes and bring your attention to the movement of your breath, its inhalations and exhalations. Make no effort to change the breath in any way. Just observe its natural rhythm.

3. Appreciate the fact that your body's existence depends on drawing air in from the external environment and releasing air back into the environment, again and again and again.

4. Reflect on the fact that your body also depends on the water that you drink and the plants and animals that you ingest as food. Each time you drink a cup of water, you are drinking the rivers and oceans of the world. When you eat a salad for lunch, it's not only lettuce but also the mineral-rich soil, sunshine, and rain that are providing nourishment.

5. See clearly that the environment within your body and the environment outside of your body are intimately related. The elements comprising your body are the very same elements that comprise rivers and mountains, trees and clouds and galaxies. There is no real separation. Appreciate this deeply as you move through your day.

Now, let's learn a bit about the origins of this spiritual tradition and meet some of its most esteemed historical figures.

Taoism's Origins and Principle Teachers

The deep historical origins of Taoist practice lie in the tribal cultures that settled along China's Yellow River about 5,000 years ago. The worldview of these people was primarily a shamanic one. They were adept at communicating with the spirits of plants, minerals, and animals. They used ritual and ecstatic dance to travel, via their subtle bodies or in the "space" of consciousness, to distant planets and galaxies. Their relationship to the natural world was intimate and direct.

Such a shamanic worldview and the practices that emerged from it made their way into various Taoist lineages. Even today, certain rituals, ceremonies, and inner alchemy techniques resonate strongly with these shamanic origins.

REAL OR MYTHOLOGICAL?

As we begin highlighting some important Taoist teachers and texts, it's worth mentioning a certain ambiguity that exists around them. Historians have questioned and continue to debate whether specific Taoist teachers had ever actually existed in history or whether they (and/or their activities) are mostly legendary.

Similar questions arise in relation to the authorship of Taoist scriptures and philosophical treatises. Were they written by just one person (the cited author)? Or were they written by many people in a more collaborative effort over an extended period of time?

In many cases, the truth is likely some combination of the two, and this is actually not a problem. Devotional histories featuring quasi-historical, semi-legendary figures and their (often exaggerated) heroic lives are part of many spiritual traditions. Their function is to inspire practitioners, and the benefit of such inspiration doesn't necessarily depend on the 100 percent historical accuracy of the stories.

This isn't to say that we should jettison all historical research—not at all! The well-honed consensus of scholars plays an important role in Taoist tradition. But there's also a place for more legendary or mythological accounts as archetypes that can nourish and inspire.

After all, no one really knows what Lao Tzu's life was like moment by moment (nor the lives of Confucius, Jesus, or Buddha, for that matter). Even if we had audio or video footage—which, of course, we don't—this would tell us nothing of Lao Tzu's subjective experience, which is at least as important as his various activities.

The point is that historical records are only one piece of the puzzle. Equally important is the unfolding of the inner fruits of Taoist practice within the most intimate "dimension" of our subjective experience. It is this vibrantly awake, timeless Presence—the innermost core of our being—that is the true treasure. This is the eternal Tao that can never be spoken yet can be encountered directly.

And now, let's meet the historical/legendary founder of Taoism: Lao Tzu.

LAO TZU: THE ANCIENT CHILD

Lao Tzu (also spelled Laozi) is considered to be the founder of Classical Taoism. The vast majority of Taoist practitioners relate to Lao Tzu as their spiritual ancestor.

Was Lao Tzu a real person? Though there's debate among scholars around this issue, it seems likely that Lao Tzu did, indeed, have a historical existence. Here's what we know:

The man who would later become known as Lao Tzu was born in 601 BCE in the southern feudal state of Ch'u. His birth name was Li Erh, and his parents belonged to China's educated upper class. As a young man, Li Erh worked as a librarian in the imperial archives.

At some point (and here's where historical fact begins to morph into myth and legend), the young Li Erh grew tired of this minor government post and/or disillusioned with China's tumultuous political scene. He quit his job as a librarian and entered a period of intense questioning and internal transformation, which catalyzed a profound spiritual awakening.

Though no one is quite sure when or why Li Erh became known instead as Lao Tzu, it most likely happened in the months or years following this dramatic metamorphosis. If Li Erh was the caterpillar, then Lao Tzu was the butterfly that emerged from the chrysalis of spiritual inquiry.

Brimming with newly revealed wisdom, Lao Tzu traveled to China's western frontier, intent on leaving the country forever and/or disappearing into the (metaphoric) land of immortality.

At the final gate stood a guardsman named Wen Tzu, who asked Lao Tzu for a teaching as a parting gift to humanity. In response to this request, Lao Tzu spoke—and Wen Tzu recorded—a 5,000-character treatise that would later become known as the *Tao Te Ching* (or simply the *Lao Tzu*, in honor of its author).

The Chinese name Lao Tzu translates as "old master" or "old sage." Lao Tzu is sometimes also referred to as the "ancient child." This speaks to the humor and playfulness, along with the wisdom, that permeate the *Tao Te Ching*.

CHUANG TZU: THE HAPPY TORTOISE

The Chinese philosopher and Taoist sage Chuang Tzu (also spelled Zhuangzi) lived about two centuries after Lao Tzu. He was born in 369 BCE in the feudal state of Song and, like Lao Tzu, received an excellent education. Chuang Tzu's writings are collected in a treatise that bears his name: the *Chuang Tzu*.

While Chuang Tzu's worldview was deeply influenced by the Taoist philosophy of Lao Tzu, it differed in certain ways. Unlike Lao Tzu, who, at least for a while, held a government post, Chuang Tzu had no interest in public office or political power. Instead, he espoused a life unfettered by social conventions, governmental regulations, and the desire for worldly wealth and success.

Lao Tzu envisioned the possibility of enlightened leadership—of social and political policies rooted in the wisdom of the Tao. In contrast, Chuang Tzu maintained that true freedom comes only from escaping the confused distractions of worldly affairs. In playful anecdotes and parables, Chuang Tzu makes clear his disdain for both governmental bureaucracy and high-minded scholarly pursuits.

In one story, for instance, Chuang Tzu addresses the question *What is true independence?* by telling the story of how he was approached one day (while he was fishing along the banks of a river) by a pair of government officials who, on behalf of the prince of Ch'u, offered him a prestigious government post. Chuang Tzu replies by referencing a "sacred tortoise," dead for some 3,000 years, whose shell the prince keeps on his altar.

Chuang Tzu asks: "Do you think that tortoise would rather be dead and have its remains thus honored, or be alive and wagging its tail in the mud?" The officials reply that of course the tortoise would prefer being alive, at which point Chuang Tzu exclaims, "Yes, exactly! Now get lost—because I too choose to remain wagging my tail in the mud."

Similarly, in the following parable, Chuang Tzu weighs in on the value of academic scholarship, echoing the sentiment expressed in the first chapter of the *Tao Te Ching*: The tao that can be spoken is not the eternal Tao. Here's the story, presumably addressed to a scholar who has now realized the limitations of conceptual knowledge:

A frog in a well cannot discuss the ocean, because he is limited by the size of his well. A summer insect cannot discuss ice, because it knows only its own season. A narrow-minded scholar cannot discuss the Tao, because he is constrained by his teachings. Now you have come out of your banks and seen the Great Ocean. You now know your own inferiority, so it is now possible to discuss great principles with you.

Both Lao Tzu and Chuang Tzu encourage an alignment with the rhythms of the natural world. They encourage us to honor, respect, enjoy, and celebrate the ever-transforming play of the elements as well as the unchanging Tao, which is their source. And they point to a type of knowledge—a *way of knowing*—that is direct, intuitive, and wholly independent of thought and language.

OTHER NOTABLE FIGURES

While Lao Tzu and Chuang Tzu are the most well known of early Taoist sages, here are a couple others worth mentioning whose names you may also come across:

Lieh Tzu. A fifth-century BCE philosopher who is often considered, along with Lao Tzu and Chuang Tzu, as a principle founder of Classical Taoism. The *Lieh Tzu* is also the name of a Taoist text attributed to Lieh Tzu. Some contemporary scholars, however, believe this text was actually compiled in the fourth century CE.

Wen Tzu. As mentioned earlier (see page 11), Wen Tzu is the legendary gatekeeper who requested the *Tao Te Ching*. His name is also the title of a book—the *Wen Tzu*—believed to contain additional teachings of Lao Tzu. Though scholars continue to debate the date of its composition, remnants of the *Wen Tzu* (copied on bamboo strips) were discovered in a tomb dated back to 55 BCE.

Taoist Texts

As you've learned already, each of the two main figures associated with classical Taoism, Lao Tzu and Chuang Tzu, left us a text comprised of their teachings. Lao Tzu's treatise is known as the *Tao Te Ching*, though it's sometimes also referred to simply as the *Lao Tzu*. Chuang Tzu's treatise is the *Chuang Tzu*.

But these are just two of literally thousands of texts belonging to the official Taoist canon, which includes not only scriptures and philosophical treatises but also commentaries, histories and genealogies, ceremonies, rituals, talismans, hymns, diagrams and illustrations, meditation and inner alchemy instructions, and biographies. In short, there are texts associated with every aspect of Taoist practice!

The Chinese name for this collection of Taoist texts is the Tao Tsang (also spelled Daozang), and, to date, there have been four versions of it.

TAO TSANG (DAOZANG): THE TAOIST CANON

In broad brushstrokes, here's how the Tao Tsang has evolved over the centuries:

The first attempt at gathering Taoist texts into an official collection happened in 400 CE. This First Tao Tsang included 1,200 scrolls.

In 748 CE, the Tang dynasty Emperor Tang Zuan-Zong ordered an expansion of the Taoist canon, which resulted in the Second Tao Tsang. This collection of Taoist texts was known as *The Exquisite Compendium of the Three Grottos* and consisted of somewhere between 3,700 and 7,300 scrolls. At the end of the Tang dynasty and during the tumultuous Five Dynasties period, this Taoist canon was largely destroyed in wars.

During the Song dynasty, the Taoist canon underwent a further revision in 1016 CE, which involved replacing some of the previously lost texts and removing others that had been added in the Tang dynasty. Upon completion of this process, some 4,500 scrolls remained in the Third Tao Tsang.

The current version of the Taoist canon was created during the Ming dynasty in 1444 CE. This is the Fourth Tao Tsang, and it includes 5,300 scrolls.

TAO TE CHING (DAODE JING)

The most widely translated of all Taoist texts is the *Tao Te Ching: The Book of the Way and Its Virtue*, which was originally composed during China's Spring and Autumn period (770 to 476 BCE).

Though this scripture is traditionally attributed to Lao Tzu, most scholars now believe that it was very likely written by more than one person.

The text is relatively brief: just 5,000 Chinese characters, divided into 81 chapters. In most English translations, it reads much more like poetry than prose.

In these 81 chapters, Lao Tzu (with an assist from his unnamed collaborators) advocates for a life lived in harmony with the rhythms and patterns of the natural world. He describes the attitudes and lifestyle of a Taoist sage and explores what makes for wise and effective leadership.

And he does his best to point, in the manner of a finger pointing to the moon, to the Tao: the invisible source of all things.

The writing in the *Tao Te Ching* is pithy and often enigmatic, filled with mystery and paradox. Its wisdom and intrigue have made it one of the most widely translated Chinese books.

The book containing the teachings of Chuang Tzu—
aptly named the *Chuang Tzu*—was composed during
China's Warring States period (475 to 221 BCE). It is organized into a total of 33 chapters. The historical Chuang
Tzu is generally credited as the sole author of at least the
first eight chapters of the text, with parts of later chapters perhaps added or revised by others.

While the *Tao Te Ching* is a series of chapters, the
Chuang Tzu is mostly a collection of anecdotes, para-
bles, and vignettes designed to convey Taoist wisdom.
In his text, Chuang Tzu advocates living as a wandering
Taoist hermit or recluse.

As mentioned earlier (see page 11), he's much
less optimistic than Lao Tzu about the potential for
designing social/political structures that faithfully reflect
Taoist ideals.

The stories contained in the *Chuang Tzu* tend to
be playful, paradoxical, and thought-provoking. They
challenge us to question cultural norms and dissolve
psychological habits that prevent us from aligning with
the Tao and expressing true freedom and creativity.

One of the most well-known of Chuang Tzu's writings is his butterfly dream parable. It goes like this:

> *Once upon a time, I, Chuang Tzu, dreamt I was a but-*
> *terfly, fluttering hither and thither, to all intents and*
> *purposes a butterfly. I was conscious only of my hap-*
> *piness as a butterfly, unaware that I was Chuang Tzu.*
> *Soon I awakened, and there I was, veritably myself*
> *again. Now I do not know whether I was then a man*
> *dreaming I was a butterfly, or whether I am now a*
> *butterfly, dreaming I am a man. Between a man and*

a butterfly there is necessarily a distinction. The transition is called the transformation of material things.

(TRANSLATION BY LIN YUTANG)

I CHING: THE BOOK OF CHANGES

The *I Ching*—translated variously as *Book of Changes* or *Classic of Changes*—is one of the most ancient and influential of Chinese philosophical texts. In its original form, it was a divination manual from China's Western Zhou period (1000 to 750 BCE). Several hundred years later (500 to 200 BCE), a series of philosophical commentaries were added to the original text.

The *I Ching* is composed of 64 hexagrams, which themselves are combinations of the eight trigrams (Chinese: *Pa-K'ua*): heaven, lake, fire, thunder, wind, water, mountain, and earth. The hexagrams represent all phenomena in the cosmos and their evolving circumstances.

By consulting the *I Ching* as an oracle—a divination tool—the Taoist practitioner receives guidance in relation to present or future life activities and decisions.

The text is consulted using either coins or (more traditionally) yarrow sticks.

The selected hexagrams offer clues on how best to align with earthly and heavenly influences in order to support the most beneficial outcomes.

While the *I Ching* is an important Taoist scripture and divination technique, its influence is not exclusive to Taoism. There are also a host of Confucian and Buddhist—along with some Christian, Jewish, and Islamic—commentaries on the *I Ching*.

Now, let's take a look at how Taoism relates to China's other principle religious traditions: Confucianism and Buddhism.

Taoism and Confucianism

Like Taoism, Confucianism is a spiritual tradition with a long and rich history and a multitude of lineages. Here, we'll provide just a brief overview of how the two traditions typically differ, along with some interesting historical instances of overlap.

In a nutshell, we might describe the essential difference between Confucian and Taoist worldviews as follows:

- Confucianism is framed by highly structured codes of cultural morality

- Taoism is rooted in nature-based wisdom, mystery, and spontaneity

For Confucius, a harmonious society was based on social etiquette and the careful adherence to social roles and codes of interpersonal behavior. Clearly articulated rites and rituals would guarantee that moral duties—toward one's family and society—were effectively carried out. And a virtuous government was one that supported this highly structured form of social engagement.

In contrast, Lao Tzu and Chuang Tzu prioritized an understanding of the patterns of the natural world as the source of individual and interpersonal harmony. For Taoist sages and philosophers, directly experiencing the relationship between ever-changing phenomena and the unchanging Tao was key to experiencing happiness. The Taoist emphasis on mystery, spontaneity, unlearning, and not-knowing can be understood, in part, as a direct rebellion against the rigidity of Confucian moral codes.

One instance of overlap between the two traditions originated in the midst of the political upheaval and chaos of China's Five Dynasties and Ten Kingdoms period (906 to 960 CE). Unsettled and disillusioned by this turmoil, a number of Confucian scholars renounced their formal positions to become Taoist hermits.

These renegade spiritual adepts came to embody a combination of Confucian ethics with a Taoist emphasis on living simply in the natural world. Some even incorporated Ch'an Buddhist meditation techniques, drawing equally from China's "three teachings" of Confucianism, Taoism, and Buddhism.

The Song dynasty (960 to 1279 CE) founding of the *Ch'üan-chen Tao* (the Way of Complete Reality) lineage can be seen as a further outgrowth of these mutual influences. While Ch'üan-chen Tao is rooted in Taoist inner alchemy, it also includes practices from Confucianism and Ch'an Buddhism.

Taoism and Buddhism

Buddhism was founded in Northeast India in the sixth century BCE by Prince Siddhartha, who, after his enlightenment, became known as Shakyamuni Buddha. The Four Noble Truths and the Eightfold Path form the basis of Buddhist practice.

The essential Buddhist teaching is that lasting happiness isn't found by looking outside of ourselves but rather by turning our attention inward and discovering our essential nature. The full realization of our true nature is called enlightenment.

In China, Taoism and Buddhism have influenced one another deeply. Most scholars agree that the first Buddhist scriptures were introduced to China toward the end of the Han dynasty. During the fifth or sixth century CE, the Buddhist monk, Bodhidharma, traveled to China, bringing Buddhist teachings with him. The interaction between these Buddhist teachings and indigenous Taoist practices gave birth to Ch'an Buddhism.

The introduction of Buddhism into China also influenced the development of Ch'üan-chen Tao (the Complete Reality lineage of Taoism). And in the Tang dynasty, court-sponsored debates between Taoist and Buddhist scholars gave birth to *Chongxuan Tao* (the Way of the Two-fold Mystery).

Both Taoist and Buddhist practice are rooted centrally in the doctrine of interdependence: seeing how phenomena never exist on their own but rather arise in constant dependence on an infinite number of causes and conditions. In Buddhism, this insight can be cultivated through mindfulness practice. In Taoism, the same insight can be accessed through ch'i kung and Taoist meditation.

TWO

Core Concepts

NOW THAT you've learned a bit about Taoism's historical origins and main teachers, it's time to dive deeper. This chapter presents some basic concepts and principles that are foundational to Taoist philosophy and practice. By becoming familiar with these terms, you'll have the language necessary to understand more fully the material presented in later chapters.

And as promised, we're circling back with some information about Taoist cosmology (how the universe came into existence) and soteriology (how a Taoist practice can catalyze deep and liberating transformation). Enjoy!

Wu Chi

In Taoist cosmology, *Wu Chi* is the eternal, timeless, undifferentiated origin of the universe. It is the unmanifest source of all phenomena. In the *Taijitu Shuo*—a traditional Taoist diagram—Wu Chi is represented visually as an empty circle.

Wu Chi and Tao are very close in meaning, and sometimes the terms are used interchangeably. The term *Wu Chi* is often used specifically in relation to *t'ai chi*—as the One that births the two.

- In Taoist cosmology, Wu Chi is primary

- The root (and equivalence) of Wu Chi is Tao

- From Wu Chi emerges *t'ai chi*: the dance of *yin* and *yang* (the primary duality)

- Yin and yang give birth to the Five Elements which, in various combinations, become the ten-thousand-things

We're getting ahead of ourselves a bit here, but I wanted to give you the overview—the big picture—before fleshing out the details.

The movement from Wu Chi to the ten-thousand-things is sometimes referred to as the "path of manifestation." And this is Taoist cosmology in a nutshell. It answers the basic question *How does something emerge from nothing?*

The movement from the ten-thousand-things back to Wu Chi can be referred to as the "path of return." And this is Taoist soteriology in a nutshell. It answers the question *How can Taoist practice relieve suffering and deliver peace, joy, and freedom?*

The path of manifestation and the path of return, in union, define the cycle of birth-and-death: how phenomena appear and then (sooner or later) disappear. Harmonizing with these natural patterns is a central component of Taoist practice.

Tao

In Taoist cosmology, Tao is the indefinable source of all existence. It is from the unchanging Tao that all phenomena emerge, like waves emerging from the ocean. It is from the infinite eternal Tao that the field of time and space is projected.

Although Tao is Taoism's ultimate principle—the underlying reality and source of all life—it is *not* a deity or spirit (as in shamanic traditions). Tao also should *not* be equated to the God of Abrahamic religions.

Even though it is the source of all things, Tao itself is invisible and ungraspable via our normal modes of perception. And this is what makes it so mysterious.

To become fully aligned with the Tao in all of our thoughts, words, and actions is the purpose of Taoist practice. Someone who has gained direct access to the Tao is known as a sage or an immortal.

The literal translation of the word *Tao* is "way" or "path." And this points to a second meaning of Tao, which is a way or path or movement through life that is aligned with the mystery and vibrant stillness of Tao.

So, it's paradoxical. Tao is both the source of all movement, and it is a "way" of moving that remains fully transparent to this source. Being a man or woman "of the Tao" means being attuned to cycles of change and transformation. It means acting gracefully, with ease and spontaneity, according to the principles of *wu-wei* (see page 30).

The plethora of books titled *The Tao of [fill in the blank]*—e.g., *The Tao of Pooh* or *The Tao of Physics*—demonstrates how popular culture has assimilated this second meaning of Tao. Pretty much any activity done well now invites a book with a similar title!

Yin-Yang

You're probably familiar with the *yin-yang* symbol—also known as the *t'ai chi* symbol. It's a circle divided into two fish-shaped halves: one white, one black. Within the white half there's a small black dot, and within the black half a small white dot.

The yin-yang symbol represents the emergence of duality from the unity of Tao. Yin and yang are the primordial feminine and masculine energies. And it is their dance, their movement within the field of time and space, that creates all phenomena—all of the objects and events of our universe.

Yin and yang are symbolic of all mental polarities—all the ways that human perception and cognition create our experience of the world. Thought, language, and perception function in relation to pairs of opposites: black/white, top/bottom, small/large, far/near, rich/poor, beautiful/ugly, dark/light, etc.

The yin-yang symbol illustrates Taoism's revolutionary way of understanding pairs of opposites. In the same way that the black side of the symbol includes a white dot and vice versa, so it is with all pairs of opposites! The pairs are always interdependent and mutually arising. Even though we call them opposites, we actually can't have one without also having the other.

It's kind of like the head and tail of a coin. When we flip the coin, it will land either heads-up or tails-up. But when we hold the coin in our hand, we're always holding both sides at the same time. A coin simply could not exist without having both a head and a tail.

In terms of Taoist cosmology, if yang is the head side of the coin and yin is the tail side of the coin, then Tao is the copper that is the actual substance of the coin. In a more traditional metaphor, yang is likened to the sunny side of a mountain and yin to its shady side. In this case, Tao would be the mountain itself.

Why does this matter? It matters when we have a strong desire for one half of a polarity and a strong revulsion to or fear of the other half. If our happiness depends on sitting only on the sunny side of the mountain, then when that sunny side inevitably transforms into shade, we suffer.

By understanding the interdependence of pairs of opposites, the Taoist practitioner avoids unnecessary suffering.

The Ten-Thousand-Things

Out of the dance of yin and yang emerge the Taoist Five Elements: earth, water, fire, metal, and wood. And combinations of these elements create the ten-thousand-things, which is Taoism's way of saying "everything that exists."

In Taoist cosmology, the ten-thousand-things represent the most differentiated aspect of the path of manifestation. All the various phenomena of existence— mountains, flowers, butterflies, trees, supernovas, ladybugs, human beings, etc.—are included in the ten-thousand-things.

Taoist practice in relation to the ten-thousand-things is twofold:

1. Becoming subtly attuned to the kaleidoscopic patterns of transformation (i.e., noticing how phenomena are continually changing and avoiding becoming overly attached to any particular form)

2. Remaining internally rooted in the stillness, quietude, and indestructibility of the unchanging Tao

The One

As we've seen, the Taoist path of manifestation originates from undifferentiated Wu Chi and ends with the ten-thousand-things. The path of return moves in the opposite direction, back to the nondual source of all phenomena (Tao and Wu Chi).

"The One" is a term used in relation to Taoist practices designed to facilitate such a return. As such, it is central to Taoist soteriology—the doctrine of liberation. True freedom and unconditional peace and happiness have everything to do with a practitioner's capacity to embrace the One.

The specific practice known variously as "holding to the One" or "embracing the One" or "keeping to the One" or "guarding the One" (Chinese: *Shou Yi)* supports the Taoist practitioner in bridging the gap between self and cosmos and, thus, aligning with the essence of Tao.

The path of return—via this practice of "holding to the One"—generally unfolds as a three-step process:

1. Step one involves intention, effort, and learning. The novice employs various techniques (e.g., meditation, martial arts, ritual) to harmonize their body, mind, and subtle energy (*ch'i*).

2. In step two, the practitioner releases all such structured approaches and enters into a kind of chaos characterized by receptivity, surrender, and unlearning.

3. In step three, the adept fully dissolves the perceived boundary between self and world, self and universe, self and cosmos. This is the final return to the One, the nondual source of all phenomena.

You'll learn more about this "embracing the One" practice in chapter four.

Te

The *Tao Te Ching,* Taoism's most well-known text, is often translated into English as *The Book of the Way and Its Virtue.* The Chinese word *Ching* translates as "book." The word *Tao* translates as "Way" (although it also refers to the source of all things).

And then, there's the word *te,* which is generally rendered as "virtue." But this can be a bit confusing because the notion of virtue presented in the *Tao Te Ching* is quite different from how many people think about virtue.

What te is *not* is a rigidly moralistic code of ethics or formal rules of conduct enforced by an outside authority.

Instead, *te* refers to:

1. The manifestation of Tao within all things

2. An inner power, strength, heart, integrity, and authenticity that arises spontaneously when we're in alignment with the Tao

When we're "holding to the One," our thoughts, words, and actions are naturally virtuous because the power/virtue of the Tao is flowing transparently through our human body-mind. When we're in perfect harmony with our original nature, te naturally shines through all our worldly activities.

In chapter 38 of the *Tao Te Ching*, Lao Tzu offers this view of Taoist virtue:

> *The highest virtue is to act without a sense of self*
> *The highest kindness is to give without a condition*
> *The highest justice is to see without a preference*
> *When Tao is lost one must learn the rules of virtue*
> *When virtue is lost, the rules of kindness*
> *When kindness is lost, the rules of justice*
> *When justice is lost, the rules of conduct*
> (TRANSLATION BY JONATHAN STAR)

For Lao Tzu, the highest form of virtue is when we're moving through the world in the mode of wu-wei—which we'll learn about now.

Wu-Wei

The idea that Taoism is primarily about learning how to relax and "go with the flow" may be an oversimplification, but there is a kernel of truth to it. And this kernel has a lot to do with wu-wei.

While sometimes translated as "non-action," more accurate renderings of wu-wei are "non-volitional action" or "action as though non-action" or "non-assertive action." If this seems deeply paradoxical . . . well, it is!

Wu-wei points to an intuitive, effortless way of moving through the world in perfect harmony with the patterns of the natural world. Wu-wei finds its way into phrases like "doing nothing yet nothing remains undone."

A contemporary analog might be something like when athletes are "in the zone" or when musicians have "found their groove." Suddenly, all those years of effortful training—the careful cultivation of various skills—are released into the background, into autopilot. Time seems to slow down, perception expands, and decision-making happens with effortless perfection. Great joy and power alike infuse the activity.

In these moments, the separation between a limited "me" and the surrounding environment has dissolved, and a larger intelligence has taken the helm. This is the essence of wu-wei.

And, as mentioned earlier (see page 30), the practitioner acting via wu-wei is embodying the highest form of virtue, which is wholly nonconceptual and arises spontaneously, moment by moment. There's no premeditation or adherence to formal ethical precepts.

Whatever unique situation may arise, we're able to respond in the way that is most beneficial, moving from a place of total surrender to the wisdom of the Tao.

Chuang Tzu offers a number of playful and inspiring vignettes describing the almost miraculous power of this sort of non-volitional action. For instance:

- An archer who never misses the target

- A swimmer able to navigate along the edge of a waterfall

- A butcher whose fluid, dance-like cutting up of an ox becomes a lesson on how best to live one's life

It's important to understand that wu-wei is not stagnant, lazy inactivity (i.e., becoming a couch potato), nor is it reckless impulsiveness (merely masquerading as true naturalness or spontaneity).

Rather, wu-wei involves acting in accordance with *tzu jan*—with how things *actually are* rather than how we wish or imagine them to be.

Tzu Jan

Closely related to wu-wei is tzu jan (also spelled *ziran*), typically translated as "self-so" or "that which is naturally so."

When we're acting in the spirit of wu-wei, we are allowing things (including, but not limited to, our human body-mind) to exist, develop, and transform without manipulation or conflict. Tzu jan points to this self-so quality of phenomena abiding in their natural state.

Consider a stream flowing from a mountaintop down to the ocean. It always finds the path of least resistance. Sometimes, this means flowing straight down the mountainside. At other times, it means gathering against a rock and moving sideways for a while before heading down again.

The stream is self-regulating. It expresses its natural form and moves spontaneously. It contains an uncontrived wisdom that requires no interference. Its best version of itself is already inherent and functioning naturally. Tzu jan is the basic principle that the Tao follows in its constantly unfolding manifest forms.

道 EVERYDAY TAOISM: AIMLESS WANDERING

One of the best ways to cultivate wu-wei is through the practice of aimless wandering. Here's how:

1. Set aside 15 to 20 minutes (or longer if you'd like). Turn off your phone and all other devices.

2. Go to a relatively quiet place that includes some natural beauty: a park, a garden, a courtyard, a forest meadow, or your own backyard.

3. Now, without any plan or premeditated destination, simply begin wandering. Let yourself be drawn naturally from place to place, guided by your interest in the moment or your intuition.

4. Let yourself walk for the simple pleasure of walking rather than as a means to a destination. Feel free to stop and look around whenever you'd like or sit down for a while. Move or be still for no reason other than because it feels right in the moment.

Once you become familiar with aimless wandering, you can bring its quality into many of your daily activities.

Wu and Yu

Wu and *yu* mean, respectively, nonbeing and being. These terms appear, for instance, in chapter 2 of the *Tao Te Ching*:

> *Being and non-being create each other.*
> *Difficult and easy support each other.*
> *Long and short define each other.*
> *High and low depend on each other.*
> *Before and after follow each other.*
>
> (TRANSLATION BY STEPHEN MITCHELL)

Wu (nonbeing) carries a sense of limitlessness, inexhaustibility, and non-differentiation. From the point of view of wu, the ten-thousand-things (i.e., all phenomena) are the same in that their origin is undifferentiated nonbeing.

Yu (being) includes the notion of differentiation. From the perspective of yu, the ten-thousand-things are distinct and recognizable. They are separate from one another and are assigned separate names.

So, what is that actual truth of the myriad things? Are they the same or are they different? Are ocean waves the same or different from one another?

What Lao Tzu is proposing here in chapter 2 of the *Tao Te Ching* is that "being and nonbeing create each other." But what does this mean?

Remember our discussion of opposites in the yin-yang section (see page 26)? In Taoism, opposites are understood to be interdependent. In this chapter, Lao Tzu is presenting several examples of this, including being and nonbeing.

As mental concepts, being and nonbeing make sense only in relation to one another, just like long/short or before/after make sense only in relation to one another.

He's also offering a clue about how best to understand the myriad things of Heaven and Earth (another Taoist way of saying "all phenomena"). And, like much in Classical Taoism, it's paradoxical.

Phenomena are both the same and different from each other, just as an ocean wave is both the same and different from other ocean waves. They are the same in the sense of sharing the molecular composition H_2O. But they also differ from one another in terms of shape, color, size, etc. So, in the end, they're neither strictly the same nor strictly different from one another.

Just so, all phenomena share a common origin (Tao) yet also appear, via our human perceptual and cognitive faculties, as being separate. In reality, phenomena can never be captured by the dualistic concepts of being and nonbeing; they remain free and mysterious, even as they fulfill their functions in the world.

P'u

Another Taoist concept that points to undifferentiated nondual reality is *p'u*—the uncarved block. In the same way that an uncarved block has the potential to become whatever shape the artist chooses, p'u refers to a state of pure creative potential.

In relation to Taoist practice, p'u is a kind of mental unity that supports alignment with the Tao. It is our original, natural, primordial state of mind that allows us to perceive clearly and directly without being caught in rigidly dualistic distinctions (right/wrong, beautiful/ugly, difficult/easy, etc.).

Before Michelangelo's *David* became the magnificent statue that it is, it was just a block of marble. While the block of marble held the potential for *David*, that potential was not yet actualized. Michelangelo could have chosen, instead, to sculp a unicorn, or an oak tree, or a rendering of Lao Tzu.

P'u is the block of marble containing infinite creative potential. In a slightly different usage, p'u carries the sense of perception that is free of prejudice and of action that's free from formal goals. In the absence of rigid preconceptions, the mind and body move naturally in ways that are aligned with the Tao.

Ch'i

Ch'i (also spelled *qi*) is a Taoist concept that's especially important to martial arts and inner alchemy practice. Its various English translations include "vital energy," "life-force energy," and "breath energy."

Ch'i is the subtle energy that permeates all of existence, including the human body. In more scientific terms, we might say that ch'i is the vibratory nature of phenomena—the tremoring fields and patterns of energy/information that physicists tell us are (at quantum levels) the true "building blocks" of everything we perceive.

You've likely seen ch'i in the context of other words, such as *ch'i kung* or *tai ch'i*. In relation to Chinese medicine, ch'i is the life-force energy that flows through the acupuncture meridians.

Ch'i also appears as one of the Three Treasures of inner alchemy, which you'll learn more about in upcoming chapters:

1. *Ching* = creative energy

2. *Ch'i* = life-force energy

3. *Shen* = spiritual energy

Ch'i is more or less equivalent to what Indian Yoga traditions call prana or Shakti. There are many other cultures that have their own words referring to this same subtle energy. While ch'i is generally invisible, it can be felt and, hence, experienced directly both inside and outside of the body.

Immortality

One of the most misunderstood aspects of Taoist practice has to do with immortality. The confusion arises, in large part, because immortality means very different things in different contexts. To begin sorting it out, here are three relevant Chinese words having to do with some aspect of immortality:

1. *Hsien-jen* (also spelled *xianren*). Immortal, fairy, or wizard

2. *Chen-jen* (also spelled *zhenren*). A perfected, true, or genuine person; a Taoist sage; or a spiritual master

3. *Pa-hsien* (also spelled *baxian*). The quasi-historical and mythological Taoist Eight Immortals

道 EVERYDAY TAOISM: FEELING THE CH'I

The word *ch'i* is used in several different ways within Taoism. Here's a way for you to experience it within your own body:

1. Find a quiet place to sit. Close your eyes, and then rub the palms of your hands together vigorously for 15 to 20 seconds.

2. Now, hold the palms of your hands close to one another—though not quite touching—in front of your chest.

3. With your eyes still closed, begin to create tiny circular movements with your two hands, keeping them very close to one another.

4. Feel the sensations in your hands and fingers. Feel into the space between your palms. What do you feel? Do your hands feel warm or cool? Do they feel heavy or light? Are you noticing pulsing, tingling, or magnetic sensations? This is the ch'i—the life-force energy—within your hands and fingers!

The term *immortal* is sometimes applied to an actual living person, sometimes to beings who exist in more subtle unseen realms, and sometimes to mythological characters. Immortality can also refer to spiritual awakening in the sense of maintaining a continuous alignment with the Tao.

This ambiguity reflects a paradox within the Taoist views of death. On the one hand, the death of the body is approached (particularly in the early Classical texts) as being no big deal—as simply one aspect of the cycles of the natural world. Birth and death—appearance and disappearance—are natural characteristics of the flow of life. As such, the Taoist sage is simply not bothered by them.

On the other hand, the body is deeply honored and respected in other areas of Taoist practice. It is cultivated and refined in order to enhance its health and longevity. Often, such cultivation includes the ingestion of herbal formulas and other dietary strategies to strengthen the various muscles, bones, organs, and tendons of the body.

Extreme versions of this have included the search for "elixirs of immortality": concoctions purported to deliver actual physical immortality. These experiments have occasionally resulted in death by poisoning, quite the ironic outcome. More measured approaches to increasing longevity tend to stick to proven Chinese herbal remedies.

There are also inner alchemy practices that involve the creation of an "immortal fetus": a consolidation of life-force energy designed specifically to survive the death of the body and continue to exist in more subtle realms.

In Taoist meditation, the most profound meaning of immortality is to "hold to the One," to discover and knowingly abide as our most essential nature, which is not separate from the eternal Tao. This form of immortality is about accessing a nondual dimension prior to space-time rather than attempting to extend the life of the body within a temporal framework.

Now that you've had a glimpse of some of Taoism's core concepts, we'll expand our focus to the principle themes addressed in Taoist teachings. You'll get to see how wu-wei, ch'i, and yin-yang are actually applied within Taoist practice.

THREE

Core Teachings

NOW, IT'S TIME to get to the heart of the matter with an exploration of Taoism's most essential teachings.

Many of these teachings have clear roots in Classical Taoism (i.e., the writings of Lao Tzu and Chuang Tzu). And others—such as the Three Treasures of inner alchemy—emerged in conjunction with later forms of Taoist practice.

Together, they represent the insight, knowledge, and practical acumen most often associated with Taoism.

Emptiness

You've already encountered the Chinese word *wu* in the previous chapter's discussions of Wu Chi (the primordial source of the universe), wu-wei (non-volitional action), and the pairing wu and yu (nonbeing and being).

So, it will likely be no surprise that wu has a variety of related meanings, including "not," "nothing," "without," "nothingness," and "nonbeing."

Standing on its own, wu is often translated as "emptiness" and points to one of Taoism's central teachings, which might be expressed colloquially as *less is more*.

This doesn't just mean that less is better than more. It goes deeper than that. The basic idea is that at the heart of any manifest form—any "thing" that we experience—there is a kind of emptiness that allows the form to actually function.

In chapter 11 of the *Tao Te Ching*, Lao Tzu provides several everyday examples of this principle:

- Consider the wheel of a chariot: While its 30 spokes are its most obvious feature, it is the empty space in the center (for the axle) that makes the wheel useful.

- Consider a clay pot: It is the empty space inside that makes the pot useful—i.e., able to hold things.

- Consider a house or apartment, made by erecting walls and then cutting out the doors and windows: It is the empty space inside that allows us to actually live in the home.

Emptiness is also used to describe the heart-mind of a Taoist adept, characterized by simplicity, quietude, patience, and ease. The thoughts, words, and actions of such a practitioner naturally align with the ineffable Tao. Why is this?

Because such inner realization is *empty* of tension-filled impulses or desires; it is *empty* of physical or psychic contractions that might temporarily obscure the natural qualities of the Tao. This absence of obscuring tensions allows the Tao's luminous vitality to become apparent.

Chuang Tzu likens the vibrantly still mind of the Taoist sage to a mirror upon which the forms of the world appear:

> *The still mind of the sage is the mirror of heaven and earth, the glass of all things. Vacancy, stillness, placidity, tastelessness, quietude, silence, and non-action—this is the level of heaven and earth, and the perfection of the Tao and its characteristics.*
> (TRANSLATION BY JAMES LEGGE)

It's important too that this is an emptiness that holds great power, but it's a subtle behind-the-scenes kind of power. It's no cause for depression (as with a nihilistic emptiness), but rather it invites a quiet joy and playful welcoming of all-that-is.

The Taoist Three Treasures

The Taoist Three Treasures (Chinese: *san-pao*) are three basic virtues associated with Taoism: compassion, simplicity, and patience.

FUN FACT

There are actually two sets of Three Treasures: (1) this one, and (2) the Three Treasures of inner alchemy (essence, vitality, and spirit) that you'll learn about later in this chapter. Sometimes, the former are referred to as the Three Jewels as a way of distinguishing them from the latter.

道 EVERYDAY TAOISM: NOTICING THE SPACE BETWEEN

Here's a simple exercise that will support you in accessing vibrant, fertile emptiness. It involves a figure-ground reversal that can be very fun to play with!

1. Whenever you'd like, make a conscious decision to notice the *space between* objects—more than the objects themselves. For instance, instead of seeing a table and a lamp, observe the space around these objects. Like a photographic negative, this space also has a certain shape (and other qualities) that we don't usually pay attention to. So, let the objects shift to the background and tune in to the space instead. Notice how this transforms your experience.

2. Once you're comfortable with seeing the space between external objects, try the same thing with the internal "objects" of your thoughts. Can you tune in to the silent gaps between the words, phrases, and sentences comprising your mind's internal chatter? What happens when you notice and rest in the silent spaces between (and behind) your mind-created content?

These Three Treasures first appear in chapter 67 of the *Tao Te Ching*, where Lao Tzu says:

I have just three things to teach:
simplicity, patience, compassion.
These three are your greatest treasures.
Simple in actions and in thoughts,
you return to the source of being.
Patient with both friends and enemies,
you accord with the way things are.
Compassionate toward yourself,
you reconcile all beings in the world.
(TRANSLATION BY STEPHEN MITCHELL)

Now, let's explore Lao Tzu's beautiful chapter more deeply by taking a look at each of the Three Treasures in turn.

COMPASSION

The Taoist virtue of compassion includes (and is sometimes translated as) kindness, love, gentleness, pity, charity, and mercy. This is basic human benevolence—a motherly love that includes oneself as well as all others.

According to Lao Tzu:

Compassionate toward yourself, you reconcile all beings in the world.

When we can feel genuine kindness and mercy toward ourselves, having compassion toward others becomes quite natural.

SIMPLICITY

The Taoist virtue of simplicity includes (and is sometimes also translated as) moderation, frugality, economy, restraint, and thriftiness. Being satisfied with a modest lifestyle, taking care to not be wasteful, and remaining free from complicated desires are all part of this kind of simplicity.

As Lao Tzu puts it:

> *Simple in actions and in thoughts, you return to the source of being.*

While it can be challenging to avoid some of the complexities of modern cultures, doing our best to maintain a spacious simplicity in our daily lives is one way to remain connected to and nourished by the "source of being"—the eternal Tao, our own innermost essence.

PATIENCE

The Taoist virtue of patience includes a sense of humility, a modesty that would never presume to put one's own interests ahead of others. The six-character Chinese phrase that conveys this virtue translates directly as "not daring to be first (i.e., ahead, in the lead, in the forefront) in the world."

As Lao Tzu reminds us:

> *Patient with both friends and enemies, you accord with the way things are.*

When we remain humble and not averse to being in the middle or back of the pack, we allow ourselves time to fully ripen. And we trust that when it is appropriate—that is, in accord with the way things are—we will bear the kind of fruit that aligns with our nature and is a benefit to ourselves and our communities alike.

These three treasures—compassion, patience, and simplicity—are virtues that can be cultivated. And they are qualities that the childlike Taoist sage tends to emanate naturally. What is the wisdom that gives birth to them? This is a question that we'll explore later.

But first, let's review how Taoism relates to morality and virtue more generally.

Morality/Virtue

As we've just discussed, the Three Treasures are the virtues most revered within Taoism. Lao Tzu himself sings their praises in chapter 67 of the *Tao Te Ching*.

But even earlier in the *Tao Te Ching*, Lao Tzu reminds us that the highest form of virtue can never be codified but rather emerges naturally when we're in alignment with the Tao. Here's that excerpt from chapter 38:

> *When the Tao is lost, there is goodness.*
> *When goodness is lost, there is morality.*
> *When morality is lost, there is ritual.*
> *Ritual is the husk of true faith,*
> *the beginning of chaos.*
>   (TRANSLATION BY STEPHEN MITCHELL)

When we're in alignment with the Tao, our actions emerge with spontaneous perfection in the spirit of wu-wei (non-volitional action). When we lose connection with the Tao, thus ensues a downward spiral from the Tao to conceptual notions of goodness, then down to structured codes of morality, and finally down to hollow rituals that Lao Tzu denounces as the mere "husk of true faith."

And yet, in later liturgical (public worship) and monastic (monks and nuns in monasteries) forms of institutionalized Taoism, aspects of virtue and morality do become more ritualized.

For instance:

- Rituals of purification and repentance (*chai*) to formally acknowledge unskillful behavior and aspire to do better in the future

- Rites of offering and cosmic renewal (*chiao*) to repair relationships between a community of practitioners and the deities to which they relate

The bottom line is that morality and virtue are approached in a wide variety of ways, depending on which form of Taoist practice one happens to be engaged in. It also may depend upon what stage of the path a specific practitioner is at. Beginners might need more structured approaches, while virtuous action might emerge spontaneously for practitioners rooted in the deepest wisdom. Here, Chuang Tzu expresses the most essential view:

Let your heart be at peace.
Watch the turmoil of beings
but contemplate their return.
If you don't realize the source,
you stumble in confusion and sorrow.
When you realize where you come from,

you naturally become tolerant,
disinterested, amused,
kindhearted as a grandmother,
dignified as a king.
Immersed in the wonder of the Tao,
you can deal with whatever life brings you,
and when death comes, you are ready.

So now, let's explore what exactly such wisdom entails.

Wisdom

One important aspect of Taoist wisdom is understanding the relationship between the microcosm of the human body-mind and the macrocosm of the cosmos as a whole, and how these two are self-similar: mirror images of one another at different scales.

By understanding their body-mind deeply, a Taoist practitioner also gains knowledge of the entire universe. And vice versa, a deep exploration of the patterns of the natural world tends automatically to reveal information about the practitioner's own body and mind.

And this is why it makes perfect sense to say that the "true body" of the Taoist adept is the entire cosmos!

What's also crucial to understand is the difference between:

1. wisdom/insight

2. conceptual knowledge

Though both of these are valued within Taoist practice, they involve two very distinct ways of knowing.

Chapter 1 of the *Tao Te Ching* famously highlights this distinction with the sentence, *"The tao that can be told is not the eternal Tao."*

"The tao that can be told" represents conceptual knowledge: what we come to understand by reading philosophical texts or scriptures or by hearing the spoken words of a teacher.

The "eternal Tao" points to a more direct, immediate, intimate, ineffable, and intuitive way of knowing that functions independently of conceptual thinking and language. To the mind, the eternal Tao remains unfathomable.

Think of a radio that can be tuned to different stations; our human body-mind can be tuned either to a conceptual-knowledge channel or to the nondual-wisdom channel.

In the following vignette, Chuang Tzu playfully alludes to the usefulness and limitations of conceptual knowledge:

The fish trap exists because of the fish. Once you've gotten the fish you can forget the trap. The rabbit snare exists because of the rabbit. Once you've gotten the rabbit, you can forget the snare. Words exist because of meaning. Once you've gotten the meaning, you can forget the words. Where can I find a man who has forgotten words so I can talk with him?

(TRANSLATED BY BURTON WATSON)

At this point, you may be wondering: How on earth do I go about accessing a way of knowing that has nothing to do with concepts, words, or thinking? That's a very good question!

Happily, there are some excellent Taoist meditation techniques designed specifically for this purpose. You've already been introduced to "holding to the One." And several others, such as "sitting and forgetting" and "fasting of the heart-mind" and "turning the light around," are equally excellent (more on these in the next chapter).

One key is to be willing to undergo a process of unlearning—to question and unravel some of the cognitive and perceptual habits that keep the conceptual cogs churning. As these calcified filters begin to dissolve, the space of not-knowing (a.k.a. nonconceptual knowing) is naturally revealed. This inner peace, pristine stillness, and vibrantly awake Presence is true wisdom.

So, conceptual learning has a place. But what makes Taoism unique is its dual emphasis on both learning and unlearning and on becoming adept at toggling back and forth between two distinct ways of knowing until they mysteriously, paradoxically become not-two.

Playfulness, Wonder, and Awe

Given the paradoxical nature of Taoist wisdom—its conceptual and nonconceptual aspects—it makes sense that playfulness and humor would be an integral part of how such wisdom is transmitted.

Since there's not a single word that in and of itself is fully going to represent or deliver the deepest wisdom, the best the Taoist sages can do is to speak in a slantwise way, employing metaphors, jokes, and images that are striking enough to "take our breath (and words!) away" and startle us into a place of childlike wonder and awe.

It may take weeks, months, or even years to unwind certain psychic or physical contractions and break free of old habits and beliefs. But unlearning and release can also happen in a single moment of aesthetic rapture, or with a deep belly-laugh from understanding a joke, or from the dizzying mental meltdown of fully grokking a paradox.

In such moments, we're left in a "space" characterized by an unspeakably sweet kind of knowing, a spaciously vivid awareness that is sometimes likened to the experience of a mute person tasting candy. The only thing that we might be able to say is *"Ahhh . . ."*

Out of such moments—these gaps between thoughts—arise a natural innocence, curiosity, and spontaneity, along with the deepest kind of contentment. If only for a moment, we are at home.

Nature

Nature plays a central role in Taoist practice. We've touched on this already quite a few times, but let's explore, once again, three ways in which a Taoist practitioner might engage with this aspect of the teaching.

SPENDING TIME IN THE NATURAL WORLD

Lao Tzu and Chuang Tzu both advocate spending lots of time wandering in the mountains, sitting on the banks of rivers, or appreciating the quiet vibrance of a forest; all of these are ways to benefit from the healing power of the natural world. This is the realm not only of Taoist hermits and recluses but of anyone seeking to align their body and mind with the fluid harmony of elemental patterns.

China's "grotto-heavens and auspicious sites" are caves and landforms especially revered for their spiritual

potency, making them ideal locations for Taoist practitioners (you'll learn more about these in the next
chapter). But any outdoor location that makes your heart
sing is perfect.

REPLACING CONDITIONED HABITS
WITH NATURALNESS

The essence of wu-wei is acting in ways that are spontaneous and free from the artifice of unexamined beliefs
and conditioned habits. This kind of "naturalness"
doesn't require living in a forest or on a mountaintop.
What it does typically require is a period of *unlearning*—
of dissolving old conditioning (from our culture,
parents, media, etc.) that rigidly structures our behavior.

There's some subtlety to identifying the kind of
"being natural" that is authentic wu-wei. What often
masquerades for naturalness, but actually isn't, is the
knee-jerk reactivity associated with conditioned habits.
Though it might feel "just natural" to punch someone
in the face after they have offended us, this kind of
behavior most likely comes from being psychologically
triggered and not from the true freedom of wu-wei.

ABIDING IN OUR NATURAL STATE

Being natural can also mean abiding in our natural state,
which is the inner peace and joy of our true nature. This
is the subjective experience that comes from aligning
ourselves with the primordial unity of the Tao.

So, these are three ways of "being natural" that are
found within Taoist practice. But contrary to a common
myth, Taoist naturalness doesn't necessarily exclude

the cultivation of specific skills. In fact, such cultivation plays a central role in many streams of Taoist practice.

Skill Cultivation

Though Classical Taoist texts emphasize going with the flow and dissolving calcified perceptual and cognitive habits, many forms of Taoist practice rely heavily on the skillful cultivation of the body and mind and of learning new mental and physical skills sometimes perfected to almost superhuman levels.

Let's have a look at the types of Taoist practice that involve the active cultivation of specific skill sets:

1. **Martial arts.** Skill cultivation is central to ch'i kung and kung fu practice. Think of Bruce Lee in *Enter the Dragon* or Jackie Chan in *Drunken Master*. At the highest levels, the application of skill can seem effortless with the martial artist "in the zone" of wu-wei. But this typically happens only after many years of training the body and mind.

2. **Inner alchemy.** The cultivation of the Three Treasures of essence (*ching*), vitality (*ch'i*), and spiritual energy (*shen*) is the heart of inner alchemy practice. At a certain point, these energies may seem to circulate automatically within the practitioner's body, but such an activation is typically the result of many years of intentional practice.

3. **Healing arts.** Acupuncture, herbal medicine, and tuina are Taoist healing arts that require many years of training—of conscious cultivation—to gain proficiency.

4. **Ritual and ceremony.** Taoist priests are trained to skillfully perform the various rituals and ceremonies that are central to their profession. The empowerment of talismans, the chanting of scripture, and the use of ritual implements (incense, musical instruments, etc.) are all skills that a Taoist priest must master.

5. **Taoist meditation.** Concentration, visualization, and the skillful modulation of the breath and vital energy (ch'i) are skills that are developed through a variety of Taoist meditation techniques. Other types of meditation, such as "holding to the One," involve the release of all technique into effortlessness.

6. **The art of leadership.** Lao Tzu himself encouraged the creation of enlightened leaders and political structures that embody Taoist principles. Doing this well involves a whole range of interpersonal and diplomatic skills.

7. **The art of divination.** Taoist divination tools such as feng shui, the *I Ching*, sand writing, and oracle bones generally require specific training in order to use them proficiently.

8. **Artistic skill.** Poetry, painting, music, and calligraphy are Taoist art forms that involve skillful cultivation. Here's one beautiful example from the Tang dynasty poet Li Po:

You ask why I make my home in the mountain forest,
and I smile, and am silent,
and even my soul remains quiet:
it lives in the other world

which no one owns.
The peach trees blossom.
The water flows.

(TRANSLATED BY SAM HAMILL)

The Three Treasures of Inner Alchemy

As mentioned above, one arena of Taoist cultivation is inner alchemy (*neidan*). It's called *inner* or *internal* alchemy to distinguish it from external alchemy, which is the creation of herbal/mineral/metallic formulas and so-called elixirs of immortality that are physically ingested by the Taoist adept.

The medicinal substances created through the practice of inner alchemy are, likewise, internal ones. They are energetic transformations that have beneficial effects. The Three Treasures of inner alchemy are primary among these internal medicines:

1. Ching: essence or creative energy

2. Ch'i: vitality or life-force energy

3. Shen: spirit or spiritual energy

In inner alchemy practice, the Taoist practitioner learns to gather, store, and skillfully circulate ching, ch'i, and shen to enhance health and unfold spiritual insight. Applying inner alchemy techniques for the purpose of spiritual awakening involves transforming essence into vitality, and then transforming vitality into spirit, and then merging spirit with emptiness: the eternal Tao.

Of particular importance in this process are three energetic fields (a.k.a. cinnabar fields, elixir fields) within the body called *tan t'iens* (also spelled *dantians*), which are located in the lower abdomen, chest, and head. Each of the three tan t'iens is home to one of the Three Treasures.

In Taoist practice, the three tan t'iens function in a way that's roughly equivalent to how the seven chakras function in Hindu yoga practice. They are locations within the subtle body that can be visualized and experienced directly.

One of the earliest practitioners of inner alchemy was Lu Tung-pin: a Tang dynasty scholar, poet, and Taoist adept. Today, Lu Tung-pin is honored as the father and patron of inner alchemy.

Health

Lao Tzu nicely sums up the Classical Taoist view on physical and emotional health in relation to spiritual insight:

> *Health is the greatest possession. Contentment is the greatest treasure. Confidence is the greatest friend. Nonbeing is the greatest joy.*

Physical health is a foundation that allows us to enjoy our human lives fully, including our various other possessions: houses, cars, bicycles, computers, canoes, etc. And the mental-emotional qualities of confidence and contentment nourish a deep sense of well-being.

So, physical and psychological health are valuable, for sure! But the greatest joy, says Lao Tzu, is non-being: the eternal Tao.

道 EVERYDAY TAOISM: THE INNER SMILE

The Inner Smile is a Classic Taoist inner alchemy practice whose benefits are as well-established by Western science as they are by the direct experience of countless practitioners. As it turns out, the simple act of smiling catalyzes a cornucopia of beneficial biochemical changes. Here's how to activate this internal pharmacy yourself:

1. Find a quiet place to sit or lie down.

2. Take a few deep, slow breaths and relax your jaw completely, as though you were saying "*ahh.*"

3. Rest your attention lightly at the bridge of your nose between your eyebrows. Then, allow the attention to drift even further back to the very center of your skull. Let it settle there gently.

4. Now, smile gently—with your entire being as well as with your mouth. To help maintain the gentle smile, you can imagine gazing into the eyes of someone you love deeply or contemplating a beautiful sunset.

5. With smile-energy gathering in your head and face, allow your eyes to become smiling-eyes. And now, imagine these smiling-eyes turning inward to gaze lovingly down into your chest to smile at your heart.

6. Smile internally at your heart, your spleen/stomach, your lungs, your kidneys, your liver, and then back to your heart, each organ, in turn, receiving a healing dose of smile-energy.

7. If you happen to have an injury or illness, send some smile-energy into that place, enveloping and infusing it with loving-kindness.

The Inner Smile practice is a beautiful and simple way to support physical and emotional health and well-being.

Both the body and the mind are everchanging, and one day they will dissolve completely like autumn leaves falling from their branches. So, it's good to maintain a clear perspective and not become overly attached to our fleeting and ephemeral human body-mind.

Now, in some later Taoist lineages—especially those employing inner alchemy or martial arts practice—the health and longevity of the body become a more central focus. The body is respected as a temple: a matrix for spiritual unfolding. And in the *Shang-ch'ing* lineage, the body is visualized as being the residence of deities. In these instances, the cultivation of physical health takes on greater significance.

But never in Taoist practice is the body considered an impediment to spiritual unfolding—something to be callously ignored, rejected, or abused with ascetic practices. Taoism honors the body and welcomes physical health.

Life and Death

For a Taoist practitioner, the relevant pairing is not so much "life and death" as it is "birth and death"—or "appearance and disappearance"—as two poles of a single cycle. Life welcomes the sprouting of a tree or the birth of a human baby. And similarly, when a tree or a human being dies, life itself does not mourn but rather just continues.

Moment by moment, an inhalation of breath is being born and then dying into the exhalation. Moment by moment, countless cells in our human body are dying and being born. This is how the body functions. And so, too, is the case with the cosmic body, which carries on regardless of the appearance or disappearance of any given form. An individual body dying is akin to the death of a single cell of our universal body: no big deal!

Like a tree or a flower or a mountain or a songbird, the human body goes through a series of transformations, commencing with birth and ending with death. So, let's allow it to move through these natural cycles with as little interference as possible. This is the Classical Taoist view.

DEPARTING SPIRITS/SOULS

There are forms of ceremonial Taoism that pay a lot of attention to what happens to the soul or spirit after death. Elaborate funeral rites are conducted to carefully escort the spirit of the departed.

There are also inner alchemy techniques for creating a so-called "immortal fetus"—into which the practitioner transfers their consciousness at the moment of the death of the body—in order to continue existing in more subtle realms.

But in large measure, the overall focus in Taoism is on balance and harmony in our life right now rather than worrying too much about what happens after the death of the body. Nurturing health, harmony, and inner peace here and now is what is valued.

In answer to the question *What happens when I die?* a Taoist might say, "Well, you go to the Tao, but you're a part of it already . . . so essentially, nothing happens."

What happens to the space inside of a clay pot when the clay pot breaks? It simply joins the space outside of the clay pot, from which it was never actually separate.

THE LOWDOWN ON IMMORTALITY

As you learned in the previous chapter, immortality doesn't have a single meaning within Taoism. At times, it can refer to the search for physical longevity using external alchemy techniques.

Immortality can also refer to the antics of the Taoist Eight Immortals, whose legendary capacities and supernatural abilities serve as mythological archetypes.

Most deeply, immortality refers to maintaining an alignment with the Tao, which means that our body doesn't have to die (or miraculously live forever) in order for us to become immortal. The only thing that needs to die is our mistaken belief in separation, the habit of seeing our human body-mind as existing separate from the ever-transforming patterns of the cosmos as a whole.

Now that you have a sense of some of Taoism's core teachings, let's explore how these teachings can be incorporated into a particular path of practice.

FOUR

Approaches to Taoist Practice

THIS CHAPTER will focus on how Taoism's central teachings are incorporated into an actual path of practice. How does a Taoist practitioner engage with these teachings on a day-to-day basis? As it turns out, there are a number of different approaches to "being a Taoist"—different paths through Taoism's vast territory.

While formal Taoist schools and lineages (which you'll learn more about in chapter six) often highlight just one of these approaches, they may also incorporate elements from one or several others.

Different Strokes for Different Folks

The path a person chooses will depend, in large part, upon their unique disposition and preferences. Some people naturally resonate with a devotional approach to spiritual practice. Others are drawn to the detailed protocols of inner alchemy or the unstructured spaciousness of free and easy wandering.

Each path has its own techniques for you to explore and experiment with. As you learn about the various possibilities, you'll notice which ones pique your interest and curiosity or feel most comfortable. Ultimately, of course, your path is uniquely your own.

The Way of Ceremony and Devotion

Many are surprised to learn that Taoism has a ceremonial aspect that includes a pantheon of deities and the performance of formal rituals. These elements bear a striking resemblance to the liturgical aspects of pretty much any other religious traditions—so what's up with this?

Isn't this totally at odds with the disdain that Lao Tzu and Chuang Tzu expressed for cultural conformity and religious conventions? More than anything else, Classical Taoism is associated with freedom from such rites and rituals.

This seeming contradiction is one expression of the diversity of Taoist practice. Once Taoism became institutionalized, with formally organized lineages, some of these lineages incorporated elaborate rituals. And thus was born the way of ceremony and devotion.

Taoist rituals and ceremonies, whether officiated by ordained Taoist priests or enacted by individual practitioners, include things like:

- Consecration of a sacred space
- Rites of purification (chai)
- Invocation of specific deities
- Offering incense to an altar (*baibai*)
- Chanting or reading of scriptures
- Prayers and other offerings
- Singing hymns and dancing
- Drums, bells, and other musical instruments
- Use of mudras (sacred hand movements)

Among the thousands of deities in the Taoist pantheon, some of the most important ones are:

- **The deified Lao Tzu:** known as Lord Lao or Lao-chun
- **The Three Purities:** a Taoist Trinity comprised of the Jade Pure One, the Supreme Pure One, and the Grand Pure One
- **The Taoist Eight Immortals:** especially Lu Tung-pin (the founder of inner alchemy)
- **The Three Officials:** the Official of Heaven, the Official of Earth, and the Official of Water, who are in charge of maintaining the records of a person's behavior on earth and controlling their life span and fate after death

THE HEART OF RITUAL AND DEVOTION

Two elements that are central to ceremonial Taoism are (1) the performance of rituals and (2) generating an attitude of devotion. So, let's look at each of these in turn.

A ritual is a structured set of *activities* whose purpose is to orient the practitioner's body-mind in a way that optimizes receptivity to sacred wisdom and power. What makes ritual activities potent is, in large part, the meaning that we attribute to them.

The corresponding *attitude* is one of devotion: enthusiastic openness and appreciation that allow something more expansive than our habitual points of view to infuse our experience.

In ceremonial Taoism, devotion is often directed toward one or several specific deities. Such deities can be related to as having an independent existence within a subtle realm and/or as being a symbolic representation of aspects of the practitioner's own mind.

Rituals can be grounding and inherently pleasurable. This goes for simple everyday rituals—like beginning your day with a cup of tea—as well as intricate ceremonies associated with a spiritual tradition. If you appreciate rituals and enjoy a devotional approach to life, then this may be the perfect path for you.

The Way of Divination

Divination involves knowing things that aren't immediately obvious. For instance, knowing what's going to happen in the future or which decisions are likely to be most beneficial.

The word *divination* is related to the word *divine*. So, we might consider divination techniques as tools for becoming divinely inspired—for seeing as though through the eyes of a deity, beyond our usual human capacities.

Like all Taoist practice, the way of divination is rooted in a close observation of patterns of change: how elements transform and relate to one another and how life-force energy tends to gather and flow. Perceiving these transformations with increasing subtlety is an integral part of divination.

But using a divination tool is not only about appreciating and aligning with the ebb and flow of the natural world. It almost always includes an immediately practical purpose: It provides information useful in guiding our actions.

Types of divination used in Taoism include:

1. *I Ching.* This is a well-known divination tool that we discussed in chapter one. The *I Ching* is consulted by tossing coins or by throwing yarrow sticks. The resulting hexagrams are interpreted with the help of a chosen commentary.

2. **Feng Shui.** This complex art and science is used to choose an auspicious location for a new home or office; to decide where to place a relative's grave; or to determine how to design a home, office, or garden.

EVERYDAY TAOISM: THE TAOIST ALTAR

Taoist rituals and ceremonies often involve the creation of an altar. And while the specifics can vary widely, there are certain objects that are almost always present and can form the basis of your own Taoist altar. Each of these objects has a specific symbolic meaning.

1. A picture or statue of the deity to be honored. Choose a deity or immortal whose qualities you feel inspired by and whom you wish to honor or emulate.

2. The Sacred Lamp. This represents the light of Tao—primordial wisdom untouched by cycles of change—and is placed in the center of the altar in front of the picture or statue. Traditionally, the Sacred Lamp remains continuously lit to represent the indestructible nature of the eternal Tao.

3. Two candles. These represent the sun (with its yang-energy) and the moon (with its yin-energy) and are placed on the left and right of the Sacred Lamp.

4. Three cups. These are placed in front of the Sacred Lamp. Each cup is filled with something different: (1) the cup on the left with water, symbolic of yang; (2) the cup on the right with tea, symbolic of yin; and (3) the cup in the center with uncooked grains of rice, symbolic of the union of yin and yang.

5. Five plates of fruit and bowls of food. These are placed in front of the cups and represent the Taoist Five Elements— wood, fire, earth, metal, and water—in both their Earlier Heaven (creative) and Later Heaven (destructive) forms.

6. An incense burner with three sticks of incense. The incense burner is placed in front of the plates and bowls and represents the lower tan t'ien—the inner alchemy cauldron in which the Three Treasures (essence, vitality, and spirit) are gathered and refined. The three sticks of incense represent these Three Treasures.

The literal translation of *feng shui* is "wind-water," the two substances whose subtle flowing nature represents how life-force energy itself (ch'i) gathers and flows. Feng shui is all about creating the most harmonious flow of ch'i in order to enhance the health and prosperity of those who inhabit the space.

3. **Sand writing.** This is also known as spirit writing or automatic writing. In this form of divination, a stick or wand, supported by a frame, is occupied by a spirit that traces words/characters in sand or on paper.

4. **Oracle bones.** This form of divination begins with writing/carving a specific question onto an animal bone. The bone is then heated until it cracks, and the cracks are interpreted (as in palm reading) for insight into the issue at hand.

5. *Kau Chim* **fortune-telling.** This practice involves shaking a bamboo cup containing 100 bamboo sticks until one of the sticks falls out. Written on each stick is a symbol corresponding to an oracle answer. Related to Kau Chim are the use of *Jiao Bei* blocks, which are used in pairs to answer yes/no questions.

Most divination techniques require some level of expertise in order to skillfully employ them. That said, it's also possible for someone with just a rudimentary understanding of the tool to experiment with it.

If you enjoy using protocols designed to enhance your perception of patterns of change—to deepen insight and/or for practical purposes—then the Way of Divination may be a good one for you.

The Way of Magic and Power

You may already be familiar with the image of a Taoist wizard, sorcerer, or magician. You've probably at least seen a couple of the Harry Potter movies, so you have some (albeit Hollywood-influenced) sense of what magic is about.

Both divination and magic provide practical tools for improving one's life. Divination involves clarifying your perception of patterns of change and influence, getting a behind-the-scenes glimpse of how things are unfolding in order to act most skillfully. Magic, on the other hand, consists of the active, intentional, and often forceful transformation of these patterns.

Instead of just peering into the mirror of destiny, the Taoist magician seeks to actively transform it. Taoist wizards and sorcerers use rituals, talismans, mudras, music, and dances of power to access subtle realms of power, invoke the assistance of spirits and deities, and transform material circumstances.

As you may recall from our chapter one discussion, Taoism's deepest historical roots are in China's shamanic cultures. And in the Way of Magic, we find clear shamanic influences. Like shamans, Taoist sorcerers engage in activities such as:

- Altering weather patterns (e.g., rainmaking)

- Combatting malevolent spirits

- Conducting exorcisms

- Offering protection and blessings

- Guiding souls of the deceased

- Traveling in their subtle spirit-body

The subtle energies that the Taoist magician invokes can be used for good or for evil purposes. This is one of the dangers of the Way of Magic. The kind of personal power that is accumulated isn't necessarily benevolent or even neutral. If you have a penchant for power and adventure—and a clear moral compass—then the Way of Magic may be perfect for you.

TALISMANS

Taoist magic frequently involves the use of talismans: strips of paper upon which specific symbols or words are drawn. Talismans are used to protect against malevolent spirits, heal the sick, and magnetize benevolent energies. Creating truly effective talismans is a skill that requires specific training.

The Way of Martial and Healing Arts

Physical health and longevity are valued aspects of Taoist practice. A strong and healthy body, along with a clear and flexible mind, are necessary starting points for many Taoist techniques. Various martial and healing arts, as well as Taoist calisthenics, are used to cultivate the body and can serve as their own path of practice.

Ch'i kung, t'ai chi ch'uan, and kung fu are just three examples of body-centered disciplines that can support health and longevity. Central to any such practice is the seamless integration of physical movement, breath, subtle energy (ch'i), and mind. A body-mind thus integrated sets the stage for overall health and well-being.

The martial arts that have the strongest connection to Taoism are those based in the Wudang monastery in Southern China. Wudang kung fu and other martial arts tend to have an internal or "soft" style, while Shaolin martial arts are more external or "hard."

External strengthening practices used by martial artists include:

- Tendon-changing: to nourish and strengthen the body's soft tissue such as muscles, tendons, ligaments, nerves, and fascia

- Marrow-washing: to nourish and strengthen the bones

- Taoist calisthenics (*Tao yin*): to develop overall strength and flexibility

Healing arts such as acupuncture, acupressure, tuina (meridian-based massage), and herbal medicine can also play a role in Taoist practice. Martial artists often avail themselves of these modalities to help prevent or recover from injury. But their benefits extend equally to all practitioners.

If you love the discipline of a martial art or feel drawn to immersing yourself in one of the healing arts, then this may be the Taoist path that's just right for you.

The Way of Inner Alchemy

As you may recall from the previous chapter, inner alchemy (neidan) practice involves the cultivation of the Three Treasures: creative energy (ching), life-force energy (ch'i), and spiritual energy (shen). Ultimately, these three "substances" or internal energies are transmuted, one into the other, resulting in a deep body-mind-spirit harmony.

The term *neidan* is often used synonymously with *ch'i kung*: life-force cultivation. While some ch'i kung forms are quite physically active, neidan is almost exclusively internal, using mind, breath, and imagery to refine life-force energy.

There are literally thousands of different inner alchemy techniques. What they tend to have in common is the use of mental focus along with the physical breathing process to beneficially affect the quality and flow of ch'i.

Practitioners of inner alchemy become adept not only at refining and circulating but also skillfully storing creative, life-force, and spiritual energy. Why is this important? Physical ailments and psychological problems are frequently the result of a disharmony or stagnation of life-force energy. But they can also be caused by a *leakage* of life-force energy. Inner alchemy practice teaches us how to avoid leaking energy and also how to access deep reservoirs of ancestral energy.

Some of the more well-known Taoist inner alchemy practices include:

- Ch'i kung standing meditation postures

- Ch'i kung walking meditation

- The microcosmic orbit

- Abdominal and vase breathing

- Absorbing energy from the natural world: earth, mountains, trees, sun, moon, stars, mist, etc.

- *Kan* and *Li* (water and fire) sexual energy transformation

If you're fascinated by the subtle energies that animate your human body-mind and feel devoted to refining these subtle energies, then the Way of Inner Alchemy may be the perfect Taoist path for you.

The Way of Mysticism and Imagination

Imagination is an incredibly powerful tool. Physicist Albert Einstein, for instance, used imagination to conduct thought experiments, such as imagining himself chasing and catching up to a beam of light, which led to his revolutionary discovery of the theory of relativity.

And imagination, which might seem to be a purely mental activity, can have immediate effects on your body. Here's a simple experiment that you can do right now to illustrate this:

Close your eyes and imagine standing in your kitchen and placing a yellow lemon on a cutting board. Imagine using a knife to cut this lemon in half, then in quarters. Now, imagine picking up one of these lemon pieces, peeling the lemon flesh away from the rind, and popping the fruit into your mouth. Imagine biting down into the piece of lemon, feeling the juice flow over your tongue, tasting its sourness.

After vividly imagining biting into a lemon, chances are good that you're now salivating even though you haven't actually been eating a lemon. This shows the power of imagination to have real effects on the human body.

There's one lineage of Taoism—*Shang-ch'ing* (Highest Purity or Supreme Clarity)—that makes extensive use of imagination. In particular, Shang-ch'ing practitioners imagine a host of deities, spirits, and immortals residing within their own bodies. These complex and detailed meditations are a tool for keeping the body healthy and protected, as well as for directly embodying the qualities of the deities.

In one Shang-ch'ing meditation, for instance, each of the Three Purities is imagined as residing in one of the three tan t'iens (energetic fields in the abdomen, chest, and head). In other meditations, practitioners imagine absorbing energies from the stars, planets, and galaxies—or traveling (in the subtle body) to these distant places.

Another mystical aspect of the Shang-ch'ing lineage (which we find also in some other Taoist schools) is its reliance upon revealed scriptures. The founder of Shang-ch'ing, Lady Wei Huacun, received as a revelation the foundational scriptures of this lineage. While this kind of "mystical download" happens within the internal space of imagination, it clearly has a different flavor than more active forms of imagination.

Artistic expression is a related aspect of the Way of Mysticism and Imagination. Poetry, painting, and calligraphy are art forms that can easily express Taoist principles such as simplicity, harmony, and a celebration of the beauty and healing power of the natural world. China's Tang dynasty is particularly renowned for the flowering of such art forms, but they are equally available to contemporary practitioners.

If you have an active imagination or a love of beauty and artistic expression, then this way of Taoist practice may suit you to perfection.

The Way of Meditation

You've already learned about several types of Taoist meditation: Shang-ch'ing meditations to place imagined deities within the body, inner alchemy meditations that use breath and subtle life-force energy, and the Taoist magician's meditations to access and manipulate subtle realms of power.

But the purpose of Taoist meditation is not only to support physical health and longevity or to access subtle realms of existence for practical benefits. Most essentially, Taoist meditation is a way of realizing our union with the eternal Tao.

The way this happens is by working directly with the mind, although breath and life-force energy also come into play. We've already discussed (in chapters two and three) the Taoist meditation known as "holding to the One." But let's just quickly review its three stages, which are also found in other Taoist meditations:

1. Stage one (associated with *yang-ch'i*) involves learning specific techniques, which are intentionally applied to help dissolve physical and psychic contractions like old conditioned habits that are no longer useful.

2. In stage two (associated with *yin-ch'i*), the Taoist initiate releases all intentional techniques and enters a space of receptivity and surrender, becoming open to grace amid what may feel like intense chaos and unknowing.

3. In stage three (the union of yin and yang), the Taoist adept experiences the dissolution of all conceptual polarities—inside/outside, self/other, etc.—in their return to the nondual source of all phenomena: the eternal Tao. This is "the One" that is then effortlessly embraced.

Other well-known Taoist meditations include:

- **Sitting and Forgetting:** follows a similar three-step process to deconstruct calcified mental and emotional habits.

- **Emptying the Mind and Filling the Belly:** overlaps with the inner alchemy practice of activating the lower tan t'ien.

- **Recovering the Real Mind:** a practice from the Ch'üan-chen Tao (Way of Complete Reality) lineage to cultivate inner stillness.

- **Fasting of the Heart-Mind:** helps identify three types of listening: (1) with the ears, (2) with the heart-mind, and (3) with the ch'i

- **Turning the Light Around:** for withdrawing our habitual external focus and resting as pure awareness (as the light of Tao)

If your motivation for Taoist practice is the cultivation of spiritual insight, then the Way of Meditation is the way to go.

道 EVERYDAY TAOISM: TURNING THE LIGHT AROUND

Turning the Light Around is a simple yet powerful Taoist meditation that you can easily explore on your own.

The "light" that's referenced here is the light of awareness—the very awareness that is aware of these words right now.

And turning this light around means withdrawing the focus of awareness from external phenomena and toward progressively more internal phenomena until, eventually, the light of awareness is shining on itself alone, like the sun illuminating only itself. Here's how:

1. Instead of paying attention to the sights and sounds of the external world, turn your attention—the light of your awareness—inward to the movement of breath in your body and other physical sensations. With your eyes closed—and preferably sitting in a relatively quiet place—feel the breath and other internal sensations for a couple of minutes.

2. Now, become aware of the awareness that's doing the noticing (of breath and physical sensation). Shine the light of awareness on awareness itself. Actually, there is just one awareness, like there's only a single brightness of the sun even as it illuminates itself.

3. Simply rest in this awareness, which is the light of Tao, shining through your human body-mind.

FUN FACT

You can learn more about Turning the Light Around from *The Secret of the Golden Flower* (translated by Thomas Cleary).

The Way of Free and Easy Wandering

This final way brings us full circle to the way of being advocated by Lao Tzu and Chuang Tzu, the original representatives of Classical Taoism.

Wandering freely through mountains and valleys, along winding rivers, and into mysterious caves, unencumbered by societal expectations, rules, and regulations—this was the way embodied by the earliest Taoists (who wouldn't even have called themselves Taoist).

China's sacred mountains and grotto-heavens (*tung-t'ien*)—underground or enclosed sacred sites such as mountain hollows, caves, and grottoes—are especially revered as auspicious locations for such aimless wandering. Wudang, Hua Shan, Jade Dragon, Huang Shan, Shaolin, Nanheng: These are the names of some of China's most sacred mountains.

But any place that inspires you can be the perfect place for wandering—for allowing naturalness, spontaneity, and innocence to emerge. Maybe it's a remote mountaintop, maybe a nearby forest, maybe a midcity park or your own backyard.

If what you value most is the cultivation of wu-wei—nonvolitional action—and the spacious, playful freedom that this engenders, then joining Lao Tzu and Chuang Tzu in their Way of Free and Easy Wandering will be the obvious choice.

The eight paths of Taoist practice that we've described here offer lots of options for engaging with Taoism's rich terrain. As for which to begin with, it's worth quoting mythologist Joseph Campbell when he famously advised, *"Follow your bliss!"*

Notice which path you're naturally drawn to and begin with that. Trust that while you bring your body-mind into greater harmony in whichever way that you choose, you will also be contributing to the harmony of your family and communities and, ultimately, to the healing of our shared planet.

FIVE

Common Myths and Misconceptions

BECAUSE TAOISM is such an amorphous spiritual tradition with a host of different lineages and techniques and a history that spans both continents and millennia, it should come as no surprise that there are misconceptions about it.

Westernized pop-culture versions of Taoism in particular can easily fall prey to beliefs and assumptions that are actually contrary to the original spirit and authentic practice of Taoism.

Let's take a look now at some of these misunderstandings with the aim of clarifying things.

As you'll see, most of these myths and misconceptions have a kernel of truth to them. Nevertheless, they also misrepresent or exclude some aspect of Taoist practice and, hence, are distortions of the truth. We'll begin with a really basic one that may surprise you.

Misconception: Lao Tzu Is the Founder of Taoism

KERNEL OF TRUTH: The *Tao Te Ching* is the earliest of what we now refer to as Classical Taoist texts. And the quasi-historical Lao Tzu most likely did write (or dictate) at least part of it. And today, the *Tao Te Ching*, attributed to Lao Tzu, is associated with a Taoist worldview more than any other text.

HOWEVER: There's a lot more to the story.

1. Lao Tzu almost certainly was not the sole author of the *Tao Te Ching*. Scholars now agree that he had collaborators and that the text as we know it today has evolved—meaning that it has been tweaked, augmented, transformed, and refined—over hundreds of years.

2. To say that Lao Tzu "founded" Taoism is not quite right, either. Why? Because during China's Classical period (when Lao Tzu was living), Taoism was never a formally organized religion. Furthermore, Lao Tzu and, even more so, Chuang Tzu, were decidedly anti-religion. They would never have intentionally set out to do something called "founding a new religion." If anything, they were advocating the dissolution of such formal societal structures.

3. The first organized Taoist religion—the *T'ien-shih Tao* (Way of the Celestial Masters)—was founded in 142 CE by Chang Tao-ling. This marks the beginning of

institutionalized Taoist practice much more than does Lao Tzu's legendary dictation of the *Tao Te Ching*.

We might wonder what Lao Tzu himself would think of being turned into a deity, placed within a pantheon, and formally worshipped. Is he now rolling in his grave or just quietly chuckling?

Misconception: Lao Tzu Wrote the *Tao Te Ching*

KERNEL OF TRUTH: Lao Tzu probably wrote at least some of the *Tao Te Ching*.

HOWEVER: As mentioned earlier (see page 86), historians now concur that the 81 chapters of the *Tao Te Ching* were almost certainly drafted by a combination of people. So, Lao Tzu definitely had help along the way.

This kind of thing happens frequently with spiritual texts, so it shouldn't be too surprising that it's true also for the *Tao Te Ching*. Across centuries or millennia, stuff gets added or deleted, either intentionally (to further a specific theological agenda) or unintentionally (when the scribe slips and makes a typo or accidently spills coffee on a section of the parchment).

It has also been conventional—in certain historical contexts—to attribute one's own writing to a more famous author-sage out of respect. This kind of reverse plagiarism makes it tricky to determine what part of the

It's notoriously difficult to translate Chinese characters into the English language. If you haven't already, check out three or four different English translations of the *Tao Te Ching* to get a sense of the wide range of possibilities. For those of us unable to read the *Tao Te Ching* in its original language, its intended meaning becomes even more slippery. Yet somehow, this text continues to have worldwide appeal. How is it that the power of a spiritual treatise, such as the *Tao Te Ching*, transcends barriers of culture and language?

scripture came directly from the original teacher and which parts were added by their disciples later on.

Misconception: Religious Taoism vs. Philosophical Taoism

KERNEL OF TRUTH: We can distinguish between (1) philosophical texts and (2) religious institutions that formally embody or espouse the principles expressed in the texts. And there are two distinct terms associated with this difference:

- Taoist philosophical texts (particularly from the Classical period) are referred to collectively as *Tao-chia* (also spelled *Daojia*)

- The organized religious institutions of Taoism are referred to as *Tao-chiao* (also spelled *Daojiao*)

HOWEVER: The texts in the Taoist canon never make this distinction in any rigid or absolute way. The two terms are largely used synonymously or interchangeably.

Pretty much every spiritual tradition has both scriptures/philosophical texts as well as some kind of institutional framework. The texts and scriptures provide a conceptual framework. They articulate theological principles and lay out philosophical arguments to support these principles.

The organizational structures provide ways of nourishing community by conducting publicly enacted rituals and ceremonies. Such institutions also train and ordain priests, distribute practical information about the tradition's beliefs and activities, and organize ways to generate financial support.

The point is that the distinction between Taoist philosophical texts and the religious institutions that have grown up around these texts is a largely artificial one. The two are so deeply intertwined that we really cannot meaningfully discuss one without also considering the other.

MORE RELEVANT DISTINCTIONS

Instead of philosophical vs. religious Taoism, the more relevant distinctions are:

1. **Classical Taoism vs. more institutionalized organized lineages.** It makes sense from a historical point of view to discuss the difference between, on the one hand, the writings of Lao Tzu and Chuang Tzu and, on the other hand, the subsequent organized lineages of Taoist practice.

   Part of this distinction has to do with the emergence of a consciously chosen and articulated Taoist identity. Lao Tzu and Chuang Tzu wouldn't have referred to themselves as Taoists. Only when Taoism became an organized religion did people begin to formally affiliate and identify themselves as Taoist.

2. **The institutional or exoteric aspect of a spiritual tradition vs. the contemplative, mystical, or esoteric aspect.** Rituals, ceremonies, scriptures, and martial arts or inner alchemy techniques comprise the external

or exoteric aspect of Taoism. The contemplative or esoteric aspect is the subjective experience of Taoist practitioners.

The difference, in a nutshell, is between (1) writing a dissertation about the history, horticulture, and biochemistry of mangos and (2) picking up a ripe mango and tasting it for yourself. While there's a connection between these two ways of knowing a mango, it's clear that writing a dissertation can never fully describe nor replace the actual experience of tasting one.

Misconception: Yin and Yang

KERNEL OF TRUTH: Taoism distinguishes between feminine energy and masculine energy—yin-ch'i and yang-ch'i—and generally values the two equally.

HOWEVER: We should avoid inferring what this may or may not mean in relation to contemporary discussions around gender and sexuality or about the role of women in organized Taoist religions.

YIN AND YANG IN TAOIST COSMOLOGY

As discussed in chapter two, yin and yang represent the primordial duality—the first perceptual/conceptual distinction to emerge out of the unified field of Wu Chi (a.k.a. the Tao).

How yin and yang and, by extension, all polarities interact with one another is represented visually by the yin-yang symbol, which shows the essence of yin within yang and vice versa. In a way, we could think of this as being Taoism's version of the Garden of Eden story. But in addition to Eve being created from one of Adam's ribs, Adam was also (and simultaneously) created from one of Eve's ribs.

So, in the context of Taoist cosmology, the relationship between masculine energy and feminine energy is used as a symbol of the relationship between any and all pairs of opposites.

YIN-CH'I AND YANG-CH'I IN INNER ALCHEMY

Yin-ch'i and yang-ch'i also appear in the context of inner alchemy, ch'i kung, and martial arts practice. It's important to understand that both yin-ch'i and yang-ch'i exist within both male and female bodies. What accounts for health and vitality for men and women alike is a harmonious relationship between masculine and feminine energy.

That said, there are certain inner alchemy practices that involve a conscious replacement of yin-ch'i with the more subtle yang-ch'i, and this is true for female as well as male practitioners.

MALE AND FEMALE DEITIES

With the rise of ceremonial Taoism came a pantheon of Taoist deities, saints, immortals, and other subtle-realm beings who became objects of worship and devotion.

Though this Taoist pantheon includes female and male deities, there is a marked imbalance in favor of deities portrayed as men. For instance, only one of the Eight Immortals is a woman.

In relation to the Taoist pantheon, then, is it fair to assume that male deities are more valued than female deities? Maybe . . . and maybe not. The Tao itself—the origin of all phenomena—is often referred to as the mother of all creation. If the source of all deities (male and female alike) is conceived of as feminine, even if a majority of the deities are masculine, then is one valued more than the other? It's hard to say.

MALE AND FEMALE TAOIST PRIESTS

Historically, there have been many more men than women who have been ordained as Taoist priests. The ratio has evened out a bit in recent years, but it still strongly favors men. This is almost certainly reflective of cultural biases and psychological patterns—forms of conditioning that make it more difficult for women to assume positions of worldly power.

While one could argue that this is a problem, Lao Tzu and Chuang Tzu would not likely have been bothered by it. In fact, they would more likely have advocated forgoing the bondage that such socially sanctioned positions entail. For women and men alike, Chuang Tzu in particular would almost certainly have encouraged the path of free and easy wandering.

ESSENCE AND FLUIDITY

The ultimate goal of Taoist meditation is to discover our nondual essence, which is beyond all polarities, including male/female and masculine/feminine. In the core of our being, we are neither woman nor man but rather the eternal Tao.

That said, the fluidity of categories represented by the yin-yang symbol, and Chuang Tzu's invitation to closely examine and challenge cultural and familial conditioning, can support us in unwinding rigidly held beliefs about gender and sexuality.

Myth: Taoists Aren't Allowed to Get Married

KERNEL OF TRUTH: There are monastic forms of Taoist practice where monks and nuns live in monasteries and remain celibate and unmarried. The most well-known form of monastic Taoism today is Ch'üan-chen Tao (also spelled *Quanzhen Dao*)—the Way of Complete Perfection.

HOWEVER: In other Taoist lineages, marriage is allowed or even required of its priests. In China's primary liturgical form of Taoism, *Cheng-I Tao* (also spelled *Zhengyi Dao*)— Orthodox Unity—monks and priests are almost always married.

And priests from the very first form of organized Taoist practice, T'ien-shih Tao (or *Tianshi Dao*)— the Way of the Celestial Masters—were also typically married and lived with their families.

So, whether or not a Taoist priest is married will depend largely on what lineage they're associated with. And there are millions of lay Taoist practitioners whose interpersonal lifestyle choices range across the whole spectrum of possibilities.

道 EVERYDAY TAOISM: DON'T BELIEVE EVERYTHING YOU THINK

When Chuang Tzu encourages us to challenge social mores and dissolve cultural conditioning, what exactly does he mean? Here's one way to engage with this sort of unlearning:

1. Don't believe everything you think!

2. Just for fun, play with questioning the script that your mind presents to you rather than automatically accepting it as fact or divine fiat.

3. Imagine that you're an actor and have been offered a role in a new movie or theatrical production. The director has sent you the script for you to peruse. Once you've read over it, you can choose whether or not to accept the role.

4. The mind's assumptions, beliefs, and interpretations are like the movie script. And you are the actor who gets to evaluate the script prior to agreeing to step into the role. You get to ask yourself, *Is this the kind of movie that I wish to be a part of?*

5. If your answer is *yes,* then step into the role and have fun. If your answer is *no thanks* then simply set that script aside and trust that a better one will be on its way soon (you may also consider becoming a scriptwriter yourself, but that's a topic for another time).

This kind of questioning will help you identify familial and cultural conditioning and begin the process of unwinding it. Remember, the starting point and basic instruction is *Don't believe everything you think!*

Myth: All Taoists Are Pacifists

The Taoist virtues of compassion, simplicity, and patience tend to engender a relaxed and generally peaceful way of being. And "going with the flow" via wu-wei and aimless wandering tend to decrease the likelihood of violently contentious encounters with other human beings.

HOWEVER: There are exceptions to this general rule, and in a way, the notion of pacifism (or any "-ism") doesn't really compute within a Taoist worldview. For instance:

- Taoist practitioners are not averse to going to battle in certain circumstances. In 184 CE, members of *T'ai-ping Tao* actively participated in the Yellow Turban Rebellion, a peasant revolt against the Chinese government.

- Parts of the *Tao Te Ching* envision what an enlightened culture and leadership might look like, and an important aspect of this vision is avoiding war and the weapons of war whenever possible. But this is not always possible.

- Sun Tzu was another sixth-century BCE Chinese Taoist philosopher who was also a renowned military strategist and general. His book, *The Art of War*, addresses precisely the issue of how to engage successfully in battle while keeping the most essential Taoist ideals intact.

- Consider also martial artists, who train specifically to be really good at fighting, capable and ready to protect themselves and their communities even if the ultimate goal of Taoist practice is internal peace and clarity.

When we observe the natural world, upon which so much Taoist practice is based, we see that it does not always appear peaceful. Yes, there are beautiful sunsets, serenely silent forests, and gently flowing rivers. But there are also hurricanes, tornadoes, and tsunamis. There are leopards chasing down, killing, and feasting on deer and antelope. There are erupting volcanoes and thunderous avalanches.

In other words, cycles of transformation witness mother nature in both wrathful and peaceful moods. So, can we say that nature is a pacifist? Does the question even make sense?

In relation to human behavior, the Classical Taoist understanding is that sometimes internal peace and clarity and perfect harmony with the Tao are expressed in ways that may not look particularly peaceful from an external point of view. Remember that spontaneously perfect action (i.e., wu-wei) doesn't abide by any preconceived rules. And since nature herself can appear in wrathful forms, so, too, can the Taoist sage.

Misconception: True Spontaneity vs. Reckless Impulsiveness

KERNEL OF TRUTH: Taoism encourages and celebrates spontaneity. This is especially true of the Classical Taoist texts attributed to Lao Tzu and Chuang Tzu.

HOWEVER: It's a mistake to confuse natural spontaneity with reckless impulsiveness or mental-emotional reactivity. The spontaneity associated with authentic Taoism is never impulsive, sloppy, irresponsible, or harmful.

Instead, it embodies effortless precision and the ability to respond with authenticity.

Genuine spontaneity arises out of openness and clarity. When we're free from rigid preconceptions and habitual physical or psychic contractions, then our human body-mind functions naturally with harmony and integrity.

Artists and athletes may experience this occasionally and refer to it as being "in the zone." Classical Taoists like Chuang Tzu suggest that it's possible to live like this more or less continuously. When we do, our thoughts, words, and actions are effortlessly beneficial. They contribute to the health and harmony of our environment and the sentient beings within it.

Misconception: True Not-Knowing vs. Spacing-Out

KERNEL OF TRUTH: Taoism values unlearning, not-knowing, and non-conceptual wisdom. We see this especially in Taoist meditation practices such as "holding to the One" and "sitting and forgetting." It's also evident in Chuang Tzu's encouragement to challenge cultural conventions and the mental-emotional habits that sustain them.

HOWEVER: It's a mistake to conclude that all Taoists are completely uninterested in conceptual knowledge.

The first stage in "holding to the One" and "sitting and forgetting" involves conceptual knowledge and the intentional application of techniques. The process of unlearning or unwinding habitual tendencies almost always requires a certain kind of effort.

Once these habit-tendencies have thinned out or fully dissolved, the "space" of not-knowing is what's left. But this newly revealed space is neither a dead void nor a collapsed or resigned nihilism. Instead, it is overflowing with vibrant awake-ness: an aware presence shining with nonconceptual clarity.

Not-knowing is also *not* about stupidity, distraction, mental dullness, sloppiness, or willful ignorance. It's not spaced-out confusion. It's not physical or intellectual laziness. There's actually a great (indefinable and ineffable) precision to it.

In true not-knowing, we contact and abide within the nonconceptual wisdom prior to thought. But this doesn't necessarily preclude the appearance of thoughts.

Consider the still depths of the ocean and the waves on its surface. The stillness of the depths is not affected by the turbulence on the surface. In the same way, we can knowingly abide within spacious stillness—as the eternal Tao—even as thought-waves are appearing on the surface of our mind.

Similarly, we can engage in intellectual pursuits, such as reading Taoist philosophy, while retaining a conscious connection to the stillness and not-knowing at the core of our being.

Myth: Inner Peace Is a Myth

KERNEL OF TRUTH: As chapter one of the *Tao Te Ching* famously reminds us:

> *The tao that can be told is not the eternal Tao.*

The term *inner peace*—or the mental concept of inner peace—is not inner peace itself. The subjective experience of inner peace can never be captured by concepts or validated scientifically. If the only truths we accept are those rooted in scientific research, then contemplative insight will forever remain nothing more than a myth.

A scientist can tell you all about the atomic structure and biochemistry of a pear. But to truly know the taste of a pear, you have to experience it yourself. Inner peace is the same.

HOWEVER: Isn't it the *experience* of inner peace and happiness that we all most deeply desire? Why would this desire even appear if not from the place that could fulfill it?

Everyone has had some experience, however fleeting, of deep inner peace, contentment, and satisfaction—a moment of feeling utterly complete. Perhaps such moments have come while listening to beautiful music, or being embraced by your beloved, or feeling awestruck by a million stars in the night sky, or even in the context of an emergency when some kind of quiet clarity emerges that allows you to resolve the situation perfectly and/or accept it fully.

What do such moments have in common? Often, our habitual mental chatter has become quiet or receded into the background. Often, our body has become relaxed, free from unnecessary tensions. And then, something we'd be tempted to call "inner peace" shines through. But any name that we give it is only a name—only a concept—and arguably no more real than a myth.

The good news, brought to you directly by Lao Tzu, is that we don't have to name it.

Now that we've cleared up some of the most common myths and misconceptions about Taoism, it's time to learn a bit more about specific Taoist lineages, which is the topic of our next chapter.

EVERYDAY TAOISM: MOMENTS OF CONTENTMENT

If the eternal Tao can never be spoken, as Lao Tzu asserts in chapter one of the *Tao Te Ching*, then how is it accessed and appreciated? One way is through natural moments of contentment, moments completely free from any sense of lack. Here's one way you can become more fully aware of such moments:

1. As you lie down to go to sleep at night, take a few minutes to reflect on the previous day. First, recall the situations in which you felt bored, agitated, tense, or stressed. As you recall these situations, have a sense of forgiving them and letting them go completely.

2. Now, bring to mind the moments that left you feeling inspired, amused, grateful, at ease, and content. Let your attention linger a bit with these moments of contentment. Simply appreciate them without trying to understand them. Let them bring a gentle smile to your face and your entire being.

3. Drift off to sleep within this energy of appreciation.

If you can make this a habit and stick with it for a couple of months, you'll likely notice the experience of inner peace becoming a more frequent visitor and eventually recognize it as your true home.

SIX

Taoist Schools and Lineages

WE BEGAN this book way back in chapter one with descriptions of the lives and teachings of Lao Tzu and Chuang Tzu, the most widely recognized of Taoist sages. The collected writings of these two teachers form the basis of Classical Taoism.

This was a very long time ago. Lao Tzu lived in the sixth century BCE and Chuang Tzu in the fourth century BCE. And neither of them made any attempt to present their wisdom-teachings formally as an official Taoist school.

Formal Taoist lineages and organizations didn't come into existence until much later. The Way of the Celestial Masters (T'ien-shih Tao), founded in 142 CE, was the first one. From that point onward, numerous other Taoist schools, sects, and lineages were created, making the landscape of organized Taoism increasingly complex.

As you'll see, each Taoist lineage has something unique to offer. There's also significant overlap with lineages borrowing teachings and techniques from one another.

The relationship between organized Taoism and the Chinese government has varied widely. In the Tang dynasty, for instance, Taoism was declared the official state religion. For this reason, many consider this to be the golden age of ceremonial Taoism.

During China's Cultural Revolution, on the other hand, the situation was pretty much the opposite. Public forms of Taoist practice were forcibly repressed and more or less eliminated (more on this in chapter seven).

For now, let's have a look at some of the most important Taoist lineages along with a few more obscure but nevertheless interesting ones. Along the way, you'll also get to meet some inspiring Taoist dignitaries, revered Taoist sages who don't often get to share the limelight with Lao Tzu and Chuang Tzu.

T'ien-shih Tao: The Way of the Celestial Masters

The Way of the Celestial Masters—T'ien-shih Tao (also spelled Tianshi Dao)—was Taoism's first organized religious community. It was founded in 142 CE by Chang Tao-ling, who, in honor of being the founder of Taoism as an organized religion, is our first Taoist dignitary.

Chang Tao-ling (also spelled Zhang Daoling) was a Taoist adept who, in 142 CE, founded and became the first spiritual leader of T'ien-shih Tao. The teachings of this community were based on a series of visionary dialogues that Chang Tao-ling had with the spirit-form of Lao Tzu.

Prior to founding T'ien-shih Tao, Chang Tao-ling was already a faith healer. And then, as the story goes, in 142 CE, he was at the summit of Heming Shan (Singing Crane Mountain) when Lao Tzu, in his subtle spirit-form, revealed to Chang the teachings that would form the basis of this new (and first) organized Taoist lineage.

Some important aspects of this teaching include:

- A newly revealed pantheon of Taoist deities, including Lao Tzu in deified form with his new name, Lao-chun (or T'ai-shang Lao-chun)

- An aspiration to create a utopian state/government based on Taoist principles that would replace the existing Chinese imperial institutions; this "new age" community was to be organized in accordance with the scriptures revealed by Lao Tzu to Chang Tao-ling

- The emergence of a great world peace (*T'ai-ping*) that would come to fruition after an apocalypse of sorts—a series of increasingly severe challenges and disasters

The development of the T'ien-shih Tao community included a hierarchy of ordained priests, codes of ethical behavior, and rituals of atonement and healing. It also included the practice of publicly reciting the chapters of the *Tao Te Ching* to honor Lao Tzu and better under-stand his teaching as well as to activate the healing power that was believed to reside in the text itself.

The honorary title of *T'ien-shih*—Heavenly or Celestial Master—was bestowed upon Chang Tao-ling as the founder and first leader of the lineage. In subsequent years, this title, along with leadership of the community,

FUN FACT

The Way of the Celestial Masters was also known as the Way of the Five Pecks (Bushels) of Rice, which is what a person was required to donate yearly as community dues and/or to receive healing from Chang Tao-ling.

was transferred to his son (Zhang Heng), and then his grandson (Zhang Lu).

Shang-ch'ing Tao: The Way of Highest Clarity

Shang-ch'ing Tao (also spelled *Shangqing Dao*) was founded about 150 years after the founding of Way of the Celestial Masters by Lady Wei Huacun. In English, this lineage is known as the Way of Highest Clarity or the Way of Supreme Purity. It is Taoism's most mystical lineage.

Like Chang Tao-ling before her, Wei Huacun received the core teachings and practices that would define this new lineage via a series of revelations. In total, 31 volumes of Taoist scripture were "downloaded" into Wei Huacan's heart-mind over a seven-year period.

Of equal importance to Wei Huacun in the creation of the Shang-ch'ing lineage was T'ao Hung-ching, who organized these voluminous revelations. One of the principle texts to emerge from this school of Taoism is *The Yellow Court Jade Classic of Internal Images of the High Pure Realm*—an inner alchemy manual that is still in use today. T'ao Hung-ching compiled the Way of Highest Clarity scriptures, making them more easily available to his community and to future Taoist practitioners. This also helped establish Shang-ch'ing Tao as a formal lineage.

Shang-ch'ing practitioners aspired to transform their human body-minds into divinely perfected beings: Taoist immortals. The tools they used were meditation, visualization, and inner alchemy. Here are some of the key features of the Way of Highest Clarity practice:

THE TAOIST BODY AND VISUALIZED DEITIES

A Shang-ch'ing practitioner uses their imagination to install an entire kingdom of deities and spirits within their human body. For instance, each of the Three Treasures (ching, ch'i, and shen) are visualized as a guardian spirit residing in its respective place within the subtle body: ching in the lower abdomen, ch'i in the chest, and shen in the head. The Tao itself is visualized as an "immortal fetus" within the lower tan t'ien.

Imagination powerfully affects the body's physiology and subtle energy. (Remember the experiment with the lemon in chapter four?) So, when these visualized spirits are vital and healthy, the practitioner's body also tends to be vital and healthy. In this way, the human body is cultivated and refined. It is honored as a temple of the divine and as a potential vehicle for immortality.

CELESTIAL REALMS: ABSORBING THE ESSENCE OF THE TAO

Along with visualizing deities within their body, the Way of Highest Clarity practitioner learns to absorb the essence of the Tao via the luminosity of the sun, moon, and stars. Clouds, mist, and dew also provide the Shang-ch'ing practitioner with a source of spiritual energy. The spirits of these heavenly bodies and earthly substances are invoked through ritual and meditation.

Shang-ch'ing practitioners also engage in "mystic flight," journeying to various celestial realms within their subtle bodies. This is one example of how a Taoist lineage was influenced by China's ancient shamanic cultures, which used similar techniques.

THE UNION OF MICROCOSM AND MACROCOSM

The ultimate goal of Shang-ch'ing practice is the experiential union of the microcosm of the human body with the macrocosm of the entire cosmos. In other words, the inside/outside polarity dissolves. The universe as a whole is perceived to be the practitioner's true body, and their true identity is recognized to be the primordial Tao. At this point, they have become an immortal.

FUN FACT

The Chinese word *Ling-pao* (Numinous Treasure) was originally used to describe a sacred object (*pao*, meaning treasure) into which a spirit (*ling*) had descended. In the case of Ling-pao Taoism, the sacred object was the human medium to receive the spiritual treasure of the newly revealed scriptures.

Ling-pao: Numinous Treasure

The Ling-pao (also spelled *Lingbao*)—Numinous Treasure—school of Taoism was based on a series of revealed texts (from the fourth and fifth centuries CE) about meditation, visualization, descriptions of heavenly realms, and the use of talismans. The Numinous Treasure school accepted the authority of the Shang-ch'ing revelations but added new revelations and scriptural innovations.

道 EVERYDAY TAOISM: VISUALIZING DEITIES IN THE BODY

One of the primary practices within the Way of Highest Clarity is visualizing deities in the body. While the official protocol involves visualizing specific Taoist deities, you can get a sense of what this kind of practice is like without having to use specifically Taoist imagery. Here's how:

1. Choose a visual symbol that you associate with health and vitality. It can be anything you'd like: a flower, a crystal or gemstone, a favorite animal, a specific shape or color, the sun or moon, a mountain, a tree, a waterfall, a rainbow, etc.

2. Close your eyes and imagine that your chosen symbol is right in front of you. Imagine it in as much detail as possible: its shape and color as well as its sound, taste, smell, and texture, if these apply.

3. Now, imagine placing a miniature version of this object somewhere within your body. If you'd like, you can place it in one of the three tan t'iens, considered especially powerful in Taoist practice: the lower abdomen, the center of the chest, or the center of the head. Or you can choose another location.

4. Vividly imagine your chosen symbol—representing health and vitality—inhabiting that place in your body like a special kind of medicine. Imagine the symbol being made of light and energy rather than dense matter. Maintain this image for a couple of minutes, and then let it dissolve. Notice how you feel and, even though the image is now gone, allow this feeling to linger.

The Ling-pao scriptures incorporated texts from a wide variety of existing traditions: from Taoist lineages such as Shang-ch'ing and T'ien-shih Tao and also from Buddhism. Its aspiration in doing so was to create a new universal religion for all of China and a new unity among Taoist practitioners. The Ling-pao writings were first compiled by the Taoist master Ge Chaofu.

Some central aspects of Numinous Treasure practice include:

- Emphasized precepts and purification

- Discouraged physical practices, such as alchemy or calisthenics, and believed that the way to immortality was via cultivation of the mind rather than focusing on the physical body

- Organized large public rituals of purification for the community

- Used protective talismans and charms in many of their rituals

- Imagined multilevel heavens and elaborate hierarchies of deities

Now, let's explore some lesser-known Taoist sects and lineages.

A Sampling of Lesser-Known Taoist Schools

So far, we've explored three Taoist traditions—the Way of the Celestial Masters, the Way of Highest Clarity, and Numinous Treasure—that have been hugely influential in shaping Taoist practice in China. Now, let's have a look at some lineages that are a bit more obscure but fascinating nonetheless. We'll begin with the Yellow Turbans.

T'AI-PING TAO: THE WAY OF GREAT PEACE (A.K.A. YELLOW TURBANS)

T'ai-ping Tao—the Way of Great Peace—was a second-century CE Taoist movement that (along with the Way of the Celestial Masters) contributed to the rise of Taoism as a formal religious tradition. It was founded by Chang Chueh, a Taoist magician-healer who sought to establish a utopian society (T'ai-ping) based on the equality of all people.

Physical healing played an important role in this type of Taoist practice. T'ai-ping Tao practitioners believed that physical illness was the result of moral wrongdoings. Resolving the illness required formal repentance, admitting the unskillful behavior, and resolving to not repeat it. This supported the practitioner in realigning with the Tao—with the natural way of things—which, in turn, fostered their physical healing.

T'ai-ping Tao community worship as well as its healing ceremonies were conducted in specially constructed and consecrated "pure chambers" (*chih shih*). The physical and moral health of each individual was understood to be deeply interwoven with the health of the community and society as a whole.

The Way of Great Peace was also known as the Yellow Turbans, and the reason for this may surprise you. This particular Taoist school participated in a political uprising against the Chinese government (Han dynasty). In 184 CE, around 300,000 T'ai-ping Tao soldiers actively engaged in the peasant revolt that became known as the Yellow Turban Rebellion.

T'AI-CHING TAO: THE WAY OF GREAT PURITY

T'ai-ching Tao (also spelled *Taiqing Dao*) was a third- to fourth-century CE Taoist school that focused on the practice of alchemy. In English, this lineage is called the Way of Great Clarity or the Way of Great Purity.

While the Way of the Celestial Masters was focused on communal living and new age beliefs (such as the creation of a "great peace" utopian culture), T'ai-ching Tao emphasized individual cultivation that included both internal and external alchemy. They experimented with the creation of herbal/mineral elixirs of immortality as well as meditation techniques for spiritual transformation.

CH'ING-WEI TAO: THE WAY OF CLARIFIED TENUITY

This unique Taoist lineage was best known for their thunder rituals (*lei-fa*) in which a Taoist priest invoked the spiritual power of thunder. Once the essence of the Tao—in the form of a thunderbolt—was fully embodied, the priest could then use this potent energy to perform healings.

T'IAN-HSIN TAO: THE WAY OF THE CELESTIAL HEART

In the same way that Ch'ing-wei Tao priests invoked the power of thunder, T'ian-hsin Tao priests invoked the spiritual power of the stars in order to perform exorcisms and healings.

CHIN-TAN TAO: THE WAY OF THE GOLDEN ELIXIR

Chin-tan Tao—the Way of the Golden Elixir—focuses almost exclusively on meditation and inner alchemy (*neidan*), the art and science of transforming and purifying the heart-mind. There's a lot of overlap between this school and Ch'üan-chen Tao—the Way of Complete Perfection—which we'll have a look at next.

In Chin-tan Tao manuals, inner alchemy is discussed in largely symbolic terms, which can make the texts a bit challenging to decipher without the assistance of a teacher. For instance, phrases such as "uniting the dragon and the tiger" appear in the instructions for specific meditations. Someone not familiar with the symbols might rightly wonder: What on earth does this mean?

It would require a Chin-tan Tao teacher to explain that a dragon symbolizes water, a tiger symbolizes fire, and the union of the dragon and tiger is the union of water and fire, which is also the union of feminine (yin) and masculine (yang) energies. And if it happens to be a green dragon in union with a

> **FUN FACT**
>
> The Chinese word *hsin* (also spelled *xin*), refers both to the physical heart as well as to emotional feelings, confidence, and trust. And because the ancient Chinese believed that the heart (rather than the brain) was the center of human intelligence and cognition, *hsin* is also sometimes translated as "mind" or "heart-mind."

white tiger, then this likely symbolizes the union of male and female practitioners engaged in dual-cultivation sexual practices.

The point is that the texts are typically cryptic and require expert assistance to decipher. One of the most revered Taoist adepts associated with Chin-tan Tao is Chang Po-tuan, an 11th-century CE Taoist adept who emphasized the dual cultivation of the body through inner alchemy practice and the mind through meditation practice.

In Taoist alchemical texts, Chin-tan Tao is sometimes used to refer to both internal and external alchemy rather than a specific school of practice.

Popular Taoist Schools

Now, let's have a look at some Taoist schools that are still going strong today both in China and in Western cultures.

CH'ÜAN-CHEN TAO: THE WAY OF COMPLETE PERFECTION

Ch'üan-chen Tao (also spelled Quanzhen Dao) is a Taoist lineage founded in 1167 CE by Wang Che. English translations of *Ch'üan-chen Tao* include the Way of Complete Perfection and the Way of Total Reality.

This school is also referred to as Northern Taoism since it flourishes mostly in Northern China as opposed to the Southern Taoism of Cheng-I Tao (the Way of Orthodox Unity). Today, the Ch'üan-chen Tao headquarters are at the White Cloud Abbey in Beijing.

Ch'üan-chen Tao is focused on inner alchemy and is primarily meditative and monastic, comprised of celibate monks and nuns living in abbeys and monasteries. Its teachings are a reinterpretation of Chin-tan Tao (the Way of the Golden Elixir) practices.

Wang Che taught that immortality can be attained within this very lifetime by entering the seclusion of a monastery, cultivating the Three Treasures (essence, vitality, and spirit), and harmonizing them with one's external life.

Key elements of the Way of Complete Perfection include:

- Emphasis on moral and spiritual discipline rather than on philosophical study or performance of ritual and ceremonies

- Emphasis on dual cultivation of body and mind through inner alchemy practice

- Incorporates aspects of Ch'an Buddhism and Confucianism; Wang Che himself was a Confucian-trained layman who gave up his government post to embark upon a path of Taoist training.

- Taoist techniques for refining the body and mind—cultivating inner quietude, health, and longevity—were integrated with the ethics of Confucianism; also added into the mix was an understanding of original mind and emptiness drawn from Ch'an Buddhism

(Buddhism's Heart Sutra even became part of the Ch'üan-chen Tao canon).

- According to Wang Che, this fusion of Taoist, Buddhist, and Confucian wisdom made possible a complete understanding of reality—hence, the name of the lineage: the Way of Complete Perfection or the Way of Total Reality.

Since its founding, Ch'üan-chen Tao has had two branches, a northern branch and a southern branch. The southern branch was led by inner alchemy adept Chang Po-tuan and advocates cultivation of the body before the mind. The northern branch was led by Chiu Chang-chun, and it advocates the cultivation of the mind before the body.

The northern branch of Ch'üan-chen Tao has become the highly organized religious tradition known as Northern Taoism that continues to flourish on mainland China (and elsewhere) today.

One of the most esteemed practitioners of Ch'üan-chen Tao was Immortal Sister Sun Bu'er—a 12th-century Taoist mystic and poet who married and had three children before devoting herself (at the age of 51) full time to Taoist practice. Eventually, she became a teacher, founded her own lineage (the Way of Purity and Tranquility), and continued to write poems expressing spiritual insight and offering friendly guidance, like this one:

Be free from grief and anxiety.
A solitary cloud and wild crane beyond constraint.
Within a thatched hut,

Leisurely read the golden books.
Forests and streams outside the window,
At the edge of the rolling hills, water and bamboo.
Luminous moon and clear wind;
Become worthy to be their companion.

(TRANSLATED BY LOUIS KOMJATHY)

LUNG-MEN: DRAGON GATE

Lung-men (Dragon Gate) is a sect of Ch'üan-chen Tao that was founded in 1656 CE by Wang Ch'ang-yüeh. Like the Way of Complete Perfection, Dragon Gate Taoism incorporates elements of both Buddhism and Confucianism, and it is based at White Cloud Abbey.

Dragon Gate offers a structured and simplified system for the practice of inner alchemy and other forms of Taoist self-cultivation.

Remember the obscure complexity of the Way of Golden Elixir meditation manuals with all their symbolic language? Practitioners such as Liu I-Ming simplified inner alchemy instructions by removing a lot of the esoteric symbolism. As the teachings became more accessible, their popularity increased in China and Western cultures alike.

Liu I-Ming was an 18th-century Taoist adept from the Dragon Gate sect who emphasized mental cultivation and understood inner alchemy to be a largely psychological process—with physical benefits that were a byproduct of psychological transformations.

Today, many Taoist temples, in Northern and Southern China alike, claim an affiliation with the Dragon Gate branch.

FUN FACT

You can learn a lot more about the Dragon Gate sect and traditional Taoist apprenticeships by reading *Opening the Dragon Gate: The Making of a Modern Taoist Wizard* by Chen Kaiguo and Zheng Shunchao (translated by Thomas Cleary). This engaging biography tells the life story of Wang Liping, the 18th-generation lineage holder of the Dragon Gate sect of the Way of Complete Perfection.

CHENG-I TAO: THE WAY OF ORTHODOX UNITY

Cheng-I Tao (the Way of Orthodox Unity) is the primary liturgical (public worship) Taoist lineage in existence today. It is active primarily in Taiwan and Southern China and, hence, is known as Southern Taoism. As you may recall from our discussion in chapter five, the priests in this form of Taoism can get married and have children.

Orthodox Unity traces its lineage all the way back to the Way of the Celestial Masters (T'ien-shih Tao)—China's first organized Taoist community. In fact, its original founding is attributed in large part to the 30th Celestial Master, Chang Chi-hsien. In the 13th century CE, Chang helped strengthen the existing Celestial Masters tradition, which would then become known as the Orthodox Unity tradition.

Just like T'ien-shih Tao, Cheng-I Tao teachings are rooted in the revelations of Lord Lao (the deified Lao Tzu) to the first Celestial Master, Chang Tao-ling. It also uses some of the teachings of the Numinous Treasure (Ling-pao) school. The emphasis in this tradition is on public worship, rituals, and ceremonies that are widely available to lay people.

Cheng-I Tao priests conduct large public ceremonies (chiao), including the rite of cosmic renewal, to harmonize the local community with the forces of the entire cosmos. These priests also conduct healing rituals,

seasonal rituals of offering and purification, and (often elaborate) funeral
rites. They may also participate in fes-
tivals associated with major Chinese
holidays, such as the Spring Festival
(Lunar New Year), the Lantern Festival, the Dragon Boat Festival, and
the Hungry Ghost Festival.

Orthodox Unity ceremonies typically involve the creation of a large
altar with images of deities and
the burning of incense. They often
employ talismans and amulets.

Overall, the practices of this Taoist
lineage most closely resemble what
is commonly thought of as "religious activity." While
the symbolism and pantheon of deities are specifically
Taoist, the ceremonies themselves are not unlike "going
to church" in any other religious tradition.

For this reason, the Orthodox Unity style of Taoist
practice can be quite surprising to people in Western
cultures whose image of Taoism is based primarily on
the teachings of Lao Tzu and Chuang Tzu.

Now that you've had a glimpse of Taoism's primary
lineages—and their most revered historical dignitaries—
let's shift the focus to Taoism today. Which of these
traditions are active in China right now? What does
Taoism look like in Western cultures? And how might
you begin your own Taoist practice? These are some of
the questions that we'll answer in the next chapter.

SEVEN

Taoism Today

NOW, LET'S take a look at Taoism today in both China and the West. What are the contours of the contemporary Taoist landscape? And what's the best way to actually enter this territory to begin practicing Taoism?

Taoism in China Today

As we've seen, Taoism's relationship with the Chinese government has shifted and changed over the millennia. Lao Tzu and Chuang Tzu were in open rebellion against political and social conventions of all kinds. The Way of the Celestial Masters (T'ien-shih Tao) envisioned a utopian society based on Taoist principles. The Yellow Turbans (T'ai-ping Tao) engaged in an actual political uprising against the Chinese government. And during the Tang dynasty, Taoism was the official state religion.

More recently, the practice of Taoism in China has been significantly disrupted by the Communist Revolution (1949) and the subsequent Cultural Revolution (1966 to 1976).

The Communist Revolution was led by Chinese revolutionary Mao Tse-tung, whose vision of a new Chinese society was informed by the principle that organized religion is the "opiate of the masses"—a phrase coined by Karl Marx.

The basic premise is that religion tends to prevent working-class people from demanding economic equality and from being willing to rise up in protest against the social and political organizations that perpetuate inequality.

TAOISM DURING THE CULTURAL REVOLUTION

The goal of the Cultural Revolution was to preserve Chinese Communism and its vision of a new modern society by purging remnants of capitalism along with anything connected to the previous more traditional Chinese culture.

In particular, anything deemed "superstitious" was rejected. And organized religion—Taoism included—was placed in this category. As a result, Taoist practices were prohibited. Many Taoist temples were destroyed, and Taoist monks, nuns, and priests were imprisoned or sent to labor camps.

During this time of the Cultural Revolution, then, public forms of Taoist practice in China were basically eliminated or pushed underground.

The good news is that, since the 1980s, Taoist practice has been resurrected within China and has also spread widely to Western cultures. The two main Taoist traditions existing in China today are Cheng-I Tao (the Way of Orthodox Unity) and Ch'üan-chen Tao (the Way of Complete Perfection). We introduced these lineages in chapter six and will review them here.

CHENG-I TAO: CHINA'S LITURGICAL TAOIST LINEAGE TODAY

Cheng-I Tao (the Way of Orthodox Unity) is the main public-worship form of Taoism in China today. This lineage is also sometimes referred to as Southern Taoism because it is found largely in South China and Taiwan. The historical roots of the Way of Orthodox Unity lie in the Way of the Celestial Masters, the very first organized Taoist community (founded in 142 CE).

Cheng-I Tao priests perform public rituals and ceremonies of all kinds, which include consecrations, offerings, purification, protection, and celebration. In preparation for these duties, Cheng-I Tao priests undergo extensive training that includes the study of:

- Taoist theology

- The Taoist pantheon of deities

- Liturgy and ritual, including the use of talismans

- Music and ceremonial dance

- Meditation and physical cultivation

Cheng-I Tao rituals and ceremonies are generally open to the public. This branch of Taoist practice bears the greatest resemblance to the public worship of other religious traditions.

CH'ÜAN-CHEN TAO: CHINA'S MONASTIC TAOIST LINEAGE TODAY

Ch'üan-chen Tao (the Way of Complete Perfection) is the primary monastic form of Taoism in China today. It is also referred to as Northern Taoism and has its headquarters at the White Cloud Abbey in Beijing.

This Taoist lineage maintains monasteries where monks and nuns live and receive training and are ordained as Taoist priests. The monks and nuns enjoy a simple and disciplined lifestyle overseen by the monastery abbot. Their days tend to be highly structured, with periods of meditation, worship, physical cultivation (e.g., ch'i kung), meals, sleep, and community work that includes tending the monastery gardens. Periods of the day are designated for complete silence. At other times, monks and nuns are encouraged to use spoken words with utmost care.

Ch'üan-chen Tao practice tends to be reserved for those committed to this kind of in-depth monastic training. For the most part, it is unknown to Westerners. One exception is the Lung-men (Dragon Gate) sect of this lineage, which incorporates elements of Confucianism and Buddhism and has become one of the largest and most widely recognized Taoist traditions in the world.

Another feature of Taoism in China today is the Chinese Taoist Association (CTA), which acts as an organizational bridge between Taoist lineages and the Chinese government. Taoist practitioners in China can register with the CTA in order to receive its official recognition and protection.

While the CTA possesses no actual religious authority, it does serve a number of useful purposes, including:

- Sponsoring Taoist forums, conferences, and symposiums

- Educating the public about Taoist history and practice

- Facilitating communication among Taoist lineages and between the lineages and the Chinese government

Now, let's explore the expansion of Taoist practice beyond the borders of China and into Western cultures.

Taoism in the West

When a spiritual tradition migrates from its country of origin to another culture, it necessarily transforms to accommodate its new circumstances. The hope is that what is most essential to the tradition remains intact and that its core principles are retained even if expressed in new ways. Has this happened with Taoism's migration to the West? Yes and no.

Many of the core principles of Classical Taoism as based upon the teachings of Lao Tzu and Chuang Tzu have been successfully transplanted. This is the form of Taoism that most people in Western cultures are familiar with.

But the more ceremonial forms of Taoism, which look a lot like what happens in a Christian church, a Jewish temple, or a Muslim mosque, remain unknown to most Westerners. In fact, Taoism is often presented in Western cultures as an atheist or agnostic philosophy rather than a religious or spiritual tradition.

IS TAOISM AN ATHEIST OR AGNOSTIC PHILOSOPHY?

Characterizing the ceremonial forms of Taoism as atheist or agnostic makes no sense because there are literally hundreds of gods in the Taoist pantheon. But what about Classical Taoism? Would Lao Tzu and Chuang Tzu have been comfortable with being labeled an atheist or agnostic?

An atheist is someone who disbelieves in the existence of gods of any kind. An agnostic is someone who reserves judgment on the issue; their feeling is that such a question (do gods exist or not?) can never be answered, so they neither have faith in nor actively disbelieve in gods.

While Taoism has an ultimate principle—namely, the Tao—this ultimate principle is definitely not a monotheistic God. Why? Because the Tao is nondual. It's never actually separate from anything or anyone. While a Taoist practitioner may seek to align their body-mind more fully with the Tao, to actualize the presence of the Tao, they would be unlikely to pray to the Tao as though it were an entirely external supernatural entity.

As a nondual spiritual tradition, Classical Taoism operates in a paradigm that's radically different from the Abrahamic traditions (Christianity, Judaism, Islam). In such a nondual paradigm, the question of believing or not-believing in gods doesn't apply. Any god or goddess or spirit we might experience or imagine is ultimately inseparable from our own essential nature.

TAOISM AND WESTERN NEW AGE BELIEFS

Classical Taoist philosophy sometimes gets mashed up with Western New Age beliefs in a way that takes it beyond anything that Lao Tzu or Chuang Tzu ever advocated. This can be true also of ch'i kung, martial arts, and healing techniques rooted in Taoism. What's authentically Taoist and what's something else is often lost.

So, in a nutshell, we might say that Western cultures have welcomed a Classical Taoist worldview much more than the more organized, ritualistic Taoist religious practices. And the Classical Taoist worldview often gets interwoven with new age beliefs and practices in ways that may compromise its authenticity.

Now, it's time for some down-to-earth advice on how to begin a Taoist practice.

How to Start Practicing Taoism

If you're ready to get your feet wet by incorporating Taoist practices into your own life, here's how to begin:

1. **Find the Way that works for you.** Revisit chapter four to get clear on which forms of Taoist practice most appeal to you.

2. **Connect with an existing Taoist school, lineage, or teacher for guidance and companionship.** If you're inspired by public-worship ceremonial Taoism, you'll probably want to find a Taoist temple where this is happening. If you want to learn ch'i kung or inner alchemy, then finding a teacher is a really good idea. And the same is true for Taoist magic and divination techniques. Expert guidance is highly recommended. Even on the Way of Free and Easy Wandering, having at least a couple companions—fellow travelers—is a good thing.

3. **Educate yourself with respect to your chosen form of practice.** Explore different translations of the *Tao Te Ching* and *Chuang Tzu*. Read various *I Ching* commentaries. Take on the challenge of deciphering the symbolism in inner alchemy manuals. Learn about the Taoist origins of Chinese medicine.

4. **Cherish your beginner's mind.** Even as you become something of an expert, maintain a willingness to learn new things and unlearn habits that are no longer useful. Be equally open to the mystery of not-knowing and the excitement of cultivating new skills and understanding.

Here are some things you can do in your everyday life that are consistent with a Taoist worldview.

BE INTELLIGENT WITH YOUR DIET

A vast majority of Taoist lineages encourage taking good care of our physical body, and this begins with healthy food. The sort of diet that works best will vary a bit from one person to the next. That said, these dietary suggestions will benefit most:

- Purchase locally grown and organic foods whenever possible.

- Think of everything that you put into your mouth as being on a poison-food-medicine spectrum; the general idea is to eliminate poisons and eat as many medicinal (i.e., super-nutritious) foods as possible.

- Toward this end, it's best to *reduce* your consumption of refined flours and sugar as well as foods containing lots of chemical preservatives and artificial flavors or colors.

- Things in the following two categories are generally toxic and can actually *poison* the human body, so do your best to *avoid them* completely:

  Artificial sweeteners such as sucralose (Splenda), saccharin (Sweet 'n Low, Sweet Twin), acesulfame-K (ACE K, Sunette, Equal Spoonful, Sweet One, Sweet 'n Safe), and aspartame (Equal, NutraSweet).

  Trans-fatty acids such as shortening, margarine, and partially hydrogenated vegetable oils that are used often in commercially fried foods and store-bought cakes and donuts.

- Now, for the fun part. Here's what you do get to eat: Start with lots and lots of veggies. Filling half of your lunch and dinner plate with vegetables is a good rule of thumb. Include the full veggie-rainbow of colors: green, red, yellow, purple, and orange. Baked, steamed, sautéed, or raw vegetables are a vital foundation for your healthy diet.

- The next element of a nourishing diet is high-quality protein: Free-range eggs, grass-fed beef, wild-caught salmon, chicken, turkey, and organic dairy products are all good options. Wild game such as deer, elk, or buffalo can also be a nice change of pace.

- Excellent vegetarian protein sources include lentils, chickpeas, mung beans, tempeh (fermented soy), sunflower seeds, chia seeds, hemp seeds, quinoa, almonds, and other nuts, along with eggs, yogurt, and cottage cheese. Be cautious with unfermented soy products (such as tofu), which are often difficult to digest.

- Make sure to include an abundance of healthy fats and oils, which are vital for the proper functioning of your brain and nervous system. Olive oil, coconut oil, sesame oil, almond oil, avocado oil, butter, and ghee are all excellent choices.

- Also include probiotics (cultured foods) in your diet every day, such as yogurt, kefir, sour cream, cottage cheese, tempeh, miso, sauerkraut, kimchi, and kombucha. Always look for the "live active cultures" label to be sure you're getting the probiotic benefits of these foods.

- Round out your healthy diet with organic whole grains—in moderation and with good variety— including oats, rice, rye, barley, quinoa, millet, and amaranth. Limit your intake of wheat and corn as much as possible, as these grains are often genetically modified and can create mucous and inflammation in the body.

- Satisfy your sweet tooth with a variety of fresh or dried organic fruit in moderation. Remember to avoid refined sugar as much as possible. Pure maple syrup, raw unfiltered honey, date sugar, molasses, brown rice syrup, barley malt syrup, and stevia leaf extract are better options for adding sweetness to tea, cereal, and baked goods.

ADDITIONAL DIETARY TIPS

1. Our digestive fire tends to be hottest at noon, which means our food is most efficiently digested at that time. Late-night dinners and midnight snacking can disrupt digestion and reduce the quality of your sleep.

2. Every few years, do an herbal intestinal cleanse (Dr. Natura is a very good one), which supports overall health and allows for proper absorption of food.

3. Be mindful of where your food comes from (green peas and sausages aren't born in the freezer section of the supermarket). Understand your place in the web of life. Be grateful to the plants and animals whose lives are given every day to support the life of your human body. Don't take them for granted.

Remember: Don't do anything extreme without expert guidance. Gradually transforming your diet by simply including more of the good stuff is the way to go.

HERBAL TEACHINGS

Herbal medicine dovetails beautifully with a healthy diet and is one aspect of Taoist external alchemy. Chinese herbal medicine can be a great option to consider for preventing and resolving illness (always best, of course, to consult with a professionally trained Chinese herbalist). Martial artists often rely on topical Chinese herbal balms and salves to help them recover from injuries, and you can do the same.

Here are two other ways you can incorporate the healing power of herbs into your daily life:

1. Replace coffee with black or green tea or with other herbal teas such as peppermint, ginger, chamomile, or tulsi. Matcha—the finely ground leaves of shade-grown tea plants—is a favorite among meditators because of its naturally high levels of the amino acid L-theanine, which supports a state of alert relaxation.

2. Consider supplementing your diet with some medicinal mushrooms. While not technically herbs, these can be very fun (and wholesome) to experiment with:

- Dried chaga mushrooms make a richly delicious tea.

- Reishi mushrooms are known for supporting the heart and enhancing spiritual insight.

- Lion's Mane can powerfully nourish the brain and entire nervous system.

- Cordyceps is often used by athletes to boost energy

As much as possible, moderate or eliminate altogether the use of pharmaceutical drugs, which are artificially created chemical compounds. In certain instances, such drugs are necessary—for instance, the anesthesia used during surgery. But in many cases, they can be at least partially replaced by Chinese herbal formulas, which offer a more holistic approach to healing and have fewer side effects.

Many pharmaceuticals are highly addictive—another reason to avoid them whenever possible. Consider, for instance, the current opiate addiction crisis faced by many contemporary Western cultures.

Is religion the "opiate of the masses"? We could debate this issue at length, though we currently have our hands full attempting to deal with the actual opiates that have become the opiate of the masses.

CH'I KUNG AND OTHER LONGEVITY EXERCISES

Do you remember the Chinese herbalist and martial artist Li Ching-Yuen, who was introduced in chapter three? He was reputed to have lived to be 256 years old. When asked what his secret was, here is the advice that he gave for achieving this remarkable physical longevity:

> *Keep a quiet heart, sit like a tortoise, walk sprightly like a pigeon, and sleep like a dog.*

Keeping a quiet heart is likely a reference to Taoist meditation techniques such as "keeping the One." Sitting like a tortoise—an animal that can both extend and fully retract its head and neck—could well refer to the Taoist practice of "turning the light around." Or perhaps it refers to the grounded stability of being so close to the earth. And sleeping like a dog—we might guess— points to the healing benefits of deep and nourishing sleep.

Walking sprightly like a pigeon is a way of moving that Li Ching-Yuen probably cultivated through ch'i kung and martial arts practice. When body, breath, and life-force energy (ch'i) become deeply integrated, the physical body transforms in ways that make it strong, supple, and light-of-foot.

You also can begin cultivating the body, breath, and life-force energy through a ch'i-kung or t'ai chi practice, if so inspired. Find a local class or an online video to get started.

While there are hundreds of different styles of ch'i-kung and t'ai chi, there are certain things that all such practices have in common:

1. **Becoming aware of the subtle body, the direct experience of the energetic vibrance of "being alive."** We learn to tune in to how the body feels from the inside, which is generally quite different from our mind's thoughts or ideas about the body; it's also different from the image that we see in the mirror. You may end up asking, both playfully and seriously, *Will my real body please stand up?* For t'ai chi and ch'i-kung practice, what's most important is the subtle body: physical sensations directly perceived.

2. **Becoming intimate with the breath as a gateway to perceiving the subtle body.** We're breathing all the time, but how often do we consciously notice and appreciate it? Every now and again, it can be useful to notice: In this moment, is my breath fast or slow, deep or shallow? Make no effort to change the breath in any way (though it may transform on its own). Just gently focus on your inhalations and exhalations for 5 or 10 minutes, like an attentive parent might lovingly observe their child playing in the backyard. Your eyes can be open or closed. Sometimes, it's easier to feel your breath with your eyes closed, but eventually, it's good to maintain your breath awareness with open eyes also.

Other daily habits that tend to enhance physical health and longevity include:

- Take a walk first thing in the morning to greet the new sun.

- Keep your circadian rhythms happy by installing f.lux (or a similar app) on all of your devices (one of many things that neither Lao Tzu nor Chuang Tzu had to worry about).

- Cultivate healthy, nourishing, and supportive human relationships with spiritual friends, a life partner, family, and communities.

- Practice gratitude and appreciation at every opportunity. Activate the internal medicine—with proven biochemical benefits—of a gentle smile.

- Cultivate an intelligent relationship with your sexual energy. One of the most revolutionary aspects of Taoist practice is its understanding of sexual energy as belonging to the ching (essence) category of the Three Treasures. In Taoist practice, sexual energy becomes a nourishing and potent medicine that can be circulated throughout the body to great benefit. Ching is the creative energy that's responsible not only for making babies but also for the creation of poems, symphonies, and entire galaxies.

MEDITATION

Chances are good that you're in the habit of brushing your teeth and flossing at least once a day. And this basic oral hygiene is a really good thing.

Meditation is like mental flossing. It helps us clear out mental-emotional debris rather than letting it fester and accumulate. It returns us to a (pearly-white!) clean slate.

Taoist practice includes finding an intelligent balance between activity and stillness/quietude. The physical body goes into its "rest and repair" mode each night when we sleep. Meditation facilitates a similar rest and repair cycle for both the mind and the body.

If we think of the body-mind as being similar to a computer, then the deep cleansing and quietude of meditation is akin to clearing your computer's cache: good to do frequently for optimal performance.

There are hundreds of different meditation techniques, and you've already been introduced to some of Taoism's best.

The most basic and essential form of meditation is resting in awareness. Turning the Light Around and

Holding to the One are Taoist meditations that include this most essential practice.

When we're resting in awareness, our primary interest is awareness itself rather than any object that we might be *aware of*. We become aware of awareness itself in the same way that the sun might become aware of its own brightness.

LIFESTYLE AND ATTITUDE

Here are some additional clues for living in harmony with the universe—some of which you've seen before, and some completely new:

- Spend time in nature. Honor and enjoy the trees, mountains, rivers, and meadows. Take action to protect the environment.

- Cultivate playfulness, spontaneity, wonder, and awe. Resurrect your childlike innocence and natural curiosity.

- Periodically unplug from your Wi-Fi devices. Shift your focus away from the external screens of your laptop, phone, or tablet and toward the internal screen of your own mind. Observe the coming and going of internal thoughts and images. Experiment with visualization practice.

- Question the authority of your mind's habitual beliefs, your theories about how things are or how they're supposed to be. Be willing to "try on" a completely different set of beliefs and assumptions just for fun.

- Have a sense of humor.

道 EVERYDAY TAOISM: FASTING OF THE HEART-MIND

In one of Chuang Tzu's parables, a teacher—playfully named Confucius—is having a conversation with one of his disciples. The disciple asks what "fasting of the heart-mind" means. The teacher says:

> Listen not with your ears but with your mind. Listen not with your mind but with your primal breath. The ears are limited to listening, the mind is limited to tallying. The primal breath, however, awaits things emptily. It is only through the Way that one can gather emptiness, and emptiness is the fasting of the mind.
>
> (TRANSLATION BY VICTOR MAIR)

Here's a more extended and interpretive rendering of the same passage by Thomas Merton:

> The goal of fasting is inner unity. This means hearing, but not with the ear; hearing, but not with the understanding; hearing with the spirit, with your whole being. The hearing that is only in the ears is one thing. The hearing of the understanding is another. But the hearing of the spirit is not limited to any one faculty, to the ear, or to the mind. Hence it demands the emptiness of all the faculties. And when the faculties are empty, then the whole being listens. There is then a

direct grasp of what is right there before you that can never be heard with the ear or understood with the mind. Fasting of the heart empties the faculties, frees you from limitation and from preoccupation. Fasting of the heart begets unity and freedom.

Later in the same story, the teacher explains the benefit of the kind of emptiness that emerges from heart-mind fasting:

Look at this window. It is nothing but a hole in the wall, but because of it the whole room is full of light. So when the faculties are empty, the heart is full of light. Being full of light, it becomes an influence by which others are secretly transformed.

Through telling this parable, Chuang Tzu is inviting us to notice three different ways of listening: (1) with the ears; (2) with the heart-mind; and (3) with the ch'i, our life-force energy.

Our ears hear sounds. Our heart-mind interprets the sounds, adding intellectual understanding and also, perhaps, an emotional reaction. Only when we listen with our ch'i— the unified field of our life-force energy, which has a direct link to shen (spirit)—are we listening most deeply with our whole being.

As you go through your day, see if you can notice these three levels of listening.

- Appreciate subtlety and mystery.
- Celebrate Taoist art forms such as poetry, painting, and calligraphy.
- Appreciate simplicity. Fully enjoy and be satisfied with what you have already, what's here right now. Downsize. Eliminate physical and mental clutter, allowing space for something new to appear or for the space itself to become more vibrant.
- This doesn't mean that you can't own and enjoy material things: houses, cars, fancy shoes, mountain bikes, etc. Just don't rely on them for true and lasting happiness—a task they simply were not designed to accomplish.

Parting Words: True Tao Living

What does a life infused with Taoist wisdom tend to look like?

- A life that is infused with the spirit and wisdom of Taoism is guided by an energy and intuitive understanding that is not bound by rigidly held beliefs or philosophical constructs.
- A life enriched by Taoist practice is comfortable with paradox.
- In a life nourished by the heart-blood of Taoism, our thoughts, words, and actions are naturally aligned with our deepest wisdom.
- To live in the spirit of Taoism is to give oneself fully to each and every activity. Athletes know this as *being in the zone*, where their actions are effortlessly

and mysteriously perfect. In Taoism, this is called wu-wei—nonvolitional action.

- To honor the essence of Taoism is to understand that the key to spiritual awakening (a.k.a. immortality or enlightenment) is self-knowledge.

- To live a Taoist life is to become fully aware of our body, mind, and world—and of awareness itself. Our presence shines more and more brightly.

- To live in alignment with the Tao is to relish the inner peace, joy, and contentment that arise within meditation or when viewing a beautiful flower or an awe-inspiring sunset.

I hope you've enjoyed this introduction to Taoism. With the overview and experiential exercises that I've provided, you now have everything you need to continue to explore this inspiring territory on your own.

As the Taoist poet Lu Ji has written:

Out of non-being, being is born;
out of silence, the writer produces a song.

Your own unique way of embodying Taoist wisdom will be the "song" that you contribute to the world. May it be harmonious!

SUGGESTED READING

Classic Texts

Find translations of Lao Tzu's *Tao Te Ching* and Chuang Tzu's *Chuang Tzu* that appeal to you. These are the foundational texts of Classical Taoism—great to have on hand and return to often.

Excellent for Beginners

The Book of The Heart: Embracing the Tao by Loy Ching-Yuen (translated by Trevor Carolan and Bella Chen). A collection of concise poetic verses, each of which offers an insightful reflection on some aspect of Taoist practice.

Awakening to the Tao by Liu I-Ming. These delightful meditative essays are rich with natural imagery and illustrate how a renowned Taoist adept uses the events of daily life to cultivate the Mind of Tao.

Opening the Dragon Gate: The Making of a Modern Taoist Wizard by Chen Kaiguo and Zheng Shunchao (translated by Thomas Cleary). An engaging tale of the life of Wang Liping—a lineage-holder within the Dragon Gate sect of the Way of Complete Reality school of Taoism. The book includes glimpses of a wide variety of Taoist practices, which are seamlessly interwoven into the narrative.

Taoist Yoga and Sexual Energy: Transforming Your Body, Mind, and Spirit by Eric Yudelove. A wonderfully accessible manual for inner alchemy practice—perfect for beginners as well as more advanced practitioners. The book includes illustrations and step-by-step instructions.

The Secret of the Golden Flower by Thomas Cleary. A classic Taoist meditation manual attributed to Taoist adept Lu Tung-pin that is presented in brief verses, along with insightful commentary. This is the text that explains the Taoist practice of "turning the light around."

Lieh-Tzu: A Taoist Guide to Practical Living by Eva Wong. A collection of stories, meditative musings, and friendly advice attributed to the fourth-century BCE Taoist sage Lieh Tzu.

For the Adventurous

All Else Is Bondage: Non-Volitional Living by Wei Wu Wei. Taoist wisdom in a Western idiom. Written in a Chuang Tzu-like style: playful dialogues and vignettes offered like fingers pointing to the moon.

APPENDIX

Wade-Giles and pinyin transliterations of Taoist terms used in this book.

Wade-Giles	pinyin	Wade-Giles	pinyin
Tao	Dao	Lu Tung Pin	Lu Dongbin
Taoist	Daoist	Tao Tsang	Daozang
te	de	tao-chia	daojia
ch'i	qi	tao-chiao	daojiao
ch'i-kung	qigong	tung-t'ien	dongtian
kung fu	gongfu	chiao	jiao
yin	yin	chai	jai
yang	yang	san-pao	sanbao
ching	jing	Ling-pao	Lingbao
shen	shen	neidan	neidan
pa-k'ua	bagua	tan-t'ien	dantian
feng shui	feng shui	Nei-ching t'u	Niejing tu
I Ching	Yijing	ch'ing-kung	qinggong
Lao Tzu	Laozi	Ch'uan-chen Tao	Quanzhen Dao
Tao Te Ching	Daodejing	Shang-ch'ing Tao	Shangqing Dao
Chuang Tzu	Zhuangzi	pi-ku	bigu
Lieh Tzu	Liezi	Wu Chi	Wuji

Wade-Giles	pinyin	Wade-Giles	pinyin
T'ai-chi	taiji	Cheng-I Tao	Zhengyi Dao
t'ai chi ch'uan	taijiquan	wu-wei	wuwei
T'ai-ching Tao	Taiqing Dao	chen-jen	zhenren
T'ien-shih	Tianshi	pa-hsien	baxian
Ti'en-shih Tao	Tianshi Dao	hsien-jen	xianren
T'ian-hsin Tao	Tianxin Dao	hsin	xin
Chin-tan Tao	Jindan Dao	chen-jen	zhenren
Chang Tao-ling	Zhang Daoling	tzu-jan	ziran
T'ai-ping Tao	Taiping Dao		

INDEX

ACKNOWLEDGMENTS

While the actual writing of a book is often a solitary activity, its images and ideas necessarily emerge from a rich network of influences. Naming each and every one of these influences would clearly be impossible, but I do wish to acknowledge—with deep bows of gratitude—the following people:

My mother, whose lifelong interest in t'ai chi and use of diet and nutrition to support health and well-being sowed fertile seeds.

Eva Wong and Li Junfeng—for their inspiring ch'i kung instruction.

Chip Chace—a mentor, friend, and brilliant healer whose presence continues to reverberate.

Lia Ottaviano, Kathy Watts, and Ryan Smernoff—for all varieties of editorial wizardry.

Association with my friend and teacher Francis Lucille continues to nourish and clarify my passion for nondual spiritual inquiry and provide the spark for creative endeavors such as this one.

And finally, deepest appreciation to mystic poets—past, present, and future—whose playful-serious speaking of the unspeakable remains an eternal source of inspiration.

ABOUT THE AUTHOR

 **Elizabeth Reninger** is a practitioner of the Taoist arts of ch'i kung, meditation, and poetry. She holds a master's degree and has explored and written widely on topics related to nondual spiritual traditions. Elizabeth currently lives in Boulder, Colorado—a great place for wandering in the mountains and enjoying tea with friends. Her previous books include *And Now the Story Lives Inside You: Poems by Elizabeth Reninger*, *Meditation Now: A Beginner's Guide*, and *End of Story: A Unified Mindfulness Approach to Emotional Healing & Transformation* (forthcoming; with Shinzen Young and Shelly Young).

Printed in the USA
CPSIA information can be obtained
at www.ICGtesting.com
LVHW050823280424
778210LV00008B/43